# The Voice Of The Child:
# A Handbook For Professionals

# The Voice Of The Child:
## A Handbook For Professionals

*Edited by*

Ron Davie, Graham Upton
and Ved Varma

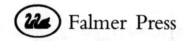 Falmer Press

(A member of the Taylor & Francis Group)
London • Washington, D.C.

**UK**    The Falmer Press, 4 John Street, London WC1N 2ET
**USA**  The Falmer Press, Taylor & Francis Inc., 1900 Frost Road, Suite 101, Bristol, PA 19007

First published in 1996

**A catalogue record for this book is available from the British Library**

**Library of Congress Cataloging-in-Publication Data are available on request**

ISBN 0 7507 0459 4 cased
ISBN 0 7507 0460 8 paper

Jacket design by Caroline Archer

Typeset in 10/12pt Bembo by
Graphicraft Typesetters Ltd., Hong Kong.

*Printed in Great Britain by Biddles Ltd., Guildford and King's Lynn on paper which has a specified pH value on final paper manufacture of not less than 7.5 and is therefore 'acid free'.*

# Contents

# Introduction: Partnership with Children: The Advancing Trend

*Ron Davie*

In October 1991 I gave the Vernon-Wall Memorial Lecture to the Education Section of the British Psychological Society under the title 'Listen to the Child' (Davie, 1993). At that time, many of my listeners had little knowledge of the 1989 Children Act and the significant shift in child law and child care practice which that Act had brought about. Courts hearing children's cases were henceforth not only to give paramountcy to the welfare of the child but also, by statute, had to have regard to 'the ascertainable wishes and feelings of the child concerned (considered in the light of his age and understanding)'.

Further, my 1991 audience was on the whole unfamiliar with the major changes of attitude and orientation in the criminal justice system in England and Wales. Criminal courts had in a few short years become significantly more child-centred. There seemed at last to be a realization that children are a very important category of witness whose testimony can improve the quality of justice if due regard is paid to their particular needs and characteristics as witnesses (Davie *op cit*; Spencer, 1990a and 1990b). In child sex abuse cases, of course, the child involved is often the **only** witness. Therefore, unless one finds a way of allowing the child to give evidence (through the use of videos, screens, etc.), whilst safeguarding the rights of the defendant, no case can be brought. This has frequently been the position in the past.

In contrast to colleagues in social work — largely but not wholly due to the impact of the 1989 Children Act and consequential guidance — my predominantly educational audience was not on the whole used to the idea that a child may have a 'right to be heard'. Nor were they necessarily committed to the concept that a child's perspective on an issue concerning him/her was (if ascertainable) always relevant and often vital to its optimal resolution. It was not that the listeners were resistant to these ideas. It was rather that the recent debates and developments in this area had mostly passed them by and that they had not really considered some of the central principles.

## The Impact of the 1994 Code of Practice

Giving a lecture on that same topic to a similar audience to-day would be a very different occasion. In particular, everyone would be very cognisant of the structure set out in the Code of Practice on the Identification and Assessment of Special Educational Needs (DFE, 1994). On the question of involving the child, the Code (para 2:35) identifies the benefits of such involvement as:

> *practical* — children have important and relevant information. Their support is crucial to the effective implementation of any individual educational programme,

> *principle* — children have a right to be heard. They should be encouraged to participate in decision-making about provision to meet their special educational needs.

A further important aspect of the acceleration of interest in, and awareness of, this issue is that the Code of Practice is a statutory instrument to which all must have regard. *All* in this context means exactly what is says, namely, that every agency, voluntary or statutory, which is concerned in the identification or assessment of a pupil with special educational needs must now take account of the principle that the child has a right to be heard.

Therefore, the Code more than any other single development or document has squarely placed the involvement of children in decision-making on the educational agenda (see Davie, 1994; Davie and Galloway, 1996), and also on the agendas of other services concerned with children's special needs, notably child health and social services. Furthermore, these latter services, at least within the context of child protection, have, since the implementation of the 1989 Children Act, been modifying their own procedures in order to ensure that the 'wishes and feelings' of children are properly considered. The combined effect of these two legislative developments has been to produce a rate of progress in this area whose momentum is discernible in terms of months rather than years.

## The Historical Context

For the above reason the task of reviewing the present position and the practical implications poses a problem as to where best to start. Perhaps it would be best to start, as they say, at the beginning by reminding ourselves that from a historical perspective, the concept of childhood itself is relatively new. Hendrick, for example, comments:

> As women have been 'hidden from history', so children have been kept from history. Prior to the 1970s very little had been written about children as people or childhood as a condition, and even at the present time there are barely half a dozen English language general histories of either focus. (1992, p.1)

If our ideas about the concept of childhood have only quite recently begun to emerge and to be put into any historical context, it is perhaps not surprising that the idea of children's rights should be one which meets with resistance. Apart from reactionary forces which are stirred by any suggestion of change, the relative unfamiliarity of the idea of children having rights independently of the adults around them (especially of their parents) can at times inhibit progress. However, any thought that this particular aspect of our topic is — if sometimes contentious — at least fairly clear and straightforward can be dismissed immediately. Any glance at Freeman's writings on children's rights will demonstrate the philosophical, not to mention legal, twists and turns to many of these issues (e.g. Freeman, 1996).

Michael Sherwin in the present book also gives an extremely helpful insight into the legal background to the child's right to be heard in particular contexts. Interestingly, too, his chapter includes a brief description of the now famous Gillick (1985) case which concerned the right of a girl under the age of 16 to receive contraceptive advice/treatment from her general practitioner without parental consent. The final judgment after appeal was that provided that children under 16 are of sufficient age and understanding they can give consent to medical treatment. This has given rise to a new phrase in the legal lexicon, namely, 'Gillick competent', which refers to a child who is judged to have such understanding.

### Practical Matters — and Problems

Without at all wishing to imply that legal issues are not practical matters — indeed at times the legal framework can be the most relevant of all the considerations — we must now pass on here to consider and review some of the day-to-day aspects of this broad topic which emerge from the following chapters and from the growing literature elsewhere.

One thing to emerge quite clearly is that listening to children — even when the general principle is accepted — often poses difficulties. As indicated above, one of the most predictable barriers is the resistance of adults — professionals included — especially when a child is thought to be exercising his/her newly given 'power' inappropriately. This is well exemplified by the headline to a *Times* newspaper article about the 1989 Children Act (Times, 17.11.92., p.33), 'Tell me off and I'll phone my lawyer'.

A not dissimilar note was struck by a child psychiatrist writing in the newsletter of a professional society to say that after a year he had become disillusioned with the new Children Act (Wolkind, 1993). Commenting on the case of a 10 year-old boy whose mother had requested that he be admitted to a psychiatric unit because he was out of her control and was felt to need a full assessment, Wolkind reported:

> The boy himself told us confidently in his interview that he had nothing to say to us, as he had instructed his lawyer to oppose the interim care order and, whether or not his mother liked it, he would be staying at home. (p.41)

Without knowing the details of the case it is impossible to comment on Wolkind's *cri de coeur* but it is inevitable that when any group of individuals is given a right, some will misuse or abuse it. (Wolkind also complained about parents' new rights under the 1989 Children Act). Children are not immune from this general tendency. However, there is no evidence that they are any more prone to it than adults. It is, of course, very galling — and sometimes tragic — when the outcome of people's abuse of their rights is to distress or harm others or themselves. However, the assumption is sometimes made (at least implicitly) that professionals themselves do not misuse their power, whereas there is well documented evidence to the contrary.

Newell's (1988) comments after the Cleveland crisis on child sex abuse are perhaps worth noting in this context. In the situation which developed in Cleveland, professionals were manifestly not listening to what the children were saying but felt themselves to be acting in the children's best interests. Newell wrote, '. . . let no-one forget after Cleveland that 'best interests' are no substitute for rights'.

## Slow to Change

In his chapter on social services' response to the 1989 Children Act, Peter Smith reminds us that professional practice and systems are often slow to change, even when new procedures are universally accepted. For example, in reviewing monitoring studies since this Act, he comments that 'More recent reports into social work in child protection continue to raise questions about social workers' tendencies not to interview children and to make assumptions about children's feelings which were not supported by the evidence'.

In her chapter Philippa Russell quotes Jackie, a young disabled pupil, whose experience indicates how far professionals — in this case teachers — have to go in listening to their pupils:

> We (pupils with special needs) want to let people know what we can
> do with our mouths, our hands, our brains. We want you to think
> about what we are saying, what we feel about things. . . . Sometimes
> they treat us like zombies, like people from another planet. But we can
> speak for ourselves.

A survey by Wade and Moore (1993) also indicates that the present situation in schools — admittedly prior to the introduction of the Code of Practice — leaves a great deal to be desired in terms of involving children. The survey found that less than a third of the mainstream teachers who responded took account of their pupils' views. On the contrary some of the teachers said they regarded this as time-consuming and of little value.

Irvine Gersch's chapter on the other hand suggests a more optimistic picture. In a survey of schools and colleges in the London borough in which he works, he found that the overwhelming majority of respondents felt that pupil involvement should be encouraged. By way of caution, however, one has to note that 60 per cent of the institutions did not respond and it may well be that those who did were not necessarily a representative sample of the borough as a whole.

Of course, one also has to have in mind with any surveys or questionnaires (and interviews, too), that some respondents may give answers which mirror what they think the researcher wants to hear. Thus, ultimately there is no substitute for observational studies, or for questionnaires which require respondents to report what they actually do rather than what they think should be done. We await these kinds of studies in the future.

### Wider Contexts

Our chapter authors are on the whole specialists dealing with problems in their clinics or departments of a kind which are not often encountered in schools, in youthwork or in normal health centres. Frequently, they are concerned with child protection work or forensic issues such as gathering evidence in interviews with children. Nevertheless, one is struck on reading their comments by how easily these translate into advice which is relevant to all child professionals in many situations. For example, Neil Hall's chapter looks in some detail at the question of children's reliability as witnesses. He also deals with the evidence on children's suggestibility. But, as he points out, there are many situations in child care, in youth justice and in assessing special educational needs where the professional must — in 'having regard to' children's views — reach a judgment as to how much weight to give these views. It may well be that reliability and suggestibility are implicit criteria in reaching that judgment. Perhaps they should be more explicit?

Another example of the more general applicability of our specialist authors' advice comes from Gill Gorrell Barnes whose suggestions about structuring an interview with a child ring true whether one is concerned with alleged sexual abuse or with, say, bullying in the playground. Kedar Dwivedi, too, raises a number of important contextual considerations of very general applicability to be borne in mind when listening to any child who comes from a different culture or subculture from one's own. These situations, Dwivedi comments, require 'sensitivity and openness to a variety of alternative communication styles and cultural perspectives'.

Thus, as Dwivedi goes on to say, a central core of our assumption in communicating with a child may be that s/he should be encouraged to believe that s/he has an independent, autonomous contribution to make to the interaction. However, it would be wrong to assume that concepts like autonomy and independence are somehow culture-free. They are inevitably influenced by the cultural context, sometimes in subtle ways. Therefore, it is important to become attuned to this context if our efforts are to have a chance of succeeding without themselves posing further problems. Gillian Pugh and Dorothy Rouse Selleck discuss this issue, too, in their chapter.

Another aspect of this wider context is tackled by Danya Glaser who amongst many other things considers the triangular system of relationships which obtains when one is interviewing both child and parents together. Cultural norms and expectations are vitally important here, too, but Glaser also points out that:

> Each of the three will have different knowledge, wishes, expectations, concerns and feelings which will influence the resultant interaction (Pearce, 1994). The child's, parents' and professional's voices do not, however, carry equal weight, and are not equally articulated, heard or acknowledged. Nor are their positions necessarily independent of each other's. In particular, the child's psychiatric disorder may well be causally related to the parent-child interaction.

If one took away the final sentence from the above quotation, it would have immediate relevance to, say, a Head of Year in a secondary school seeing a boy and his parents' about some pastoral problem which had been emerging in school; or to a discussion with a careers officer; or to an interview with a health visitor or practice nurse about the child's eating problems.

## The Age of the Child

An issue which quite frequently impinges on discussions about involving children or giving due weight to their viewpoints is their age. It is clear from Michael Sherwin's consideration of the 'Gillick competent' child that courts are now coming round to the view that the child's age per se is unimportant. What is important is the extent to which s/he understands the issues involved. This is a facet of what was referred to above as a more 'child-centred' approach on the part of courts. This, it has to be said, is a fairly recent conversion but nonetheless welcome for that. Until only a few years ago the question of the admissibility of children's evidence in criminal cases had tended to be bogged down by abstract considerations such as whether the child understood the nature of truth or the implication of taking an oath.

This movement on the part of the criminal justice system has been paralleled, as we have seen, by movement elsewhere in the law, notably, in the 1989 Children Act which refers to 'age and understanding' as qualifying factors which the court should take into account in having regard to the wishes and feelings of the child. Where there is a guardian ad litem, one of his/her principal functions may be to advise the court on this matter, sometimes with the additional help of an 'expert witness' in a difficult case.

Looking beyond the courts, is there any age below which it seems inappropriate to consider listening to the child? The straight answer to that has to be No. As both Euan Ross in his chapter — and Gillian Pugh and Dorothy

Rouse Selleck in theirs — make clear, 'listening to the child' should not be narrowly construed as being confined to speech. The 'voice of the child' includes other vocal — and indeed non-vocal — communications. This is true even of the older child, whose body language, actions and behaviour may tell as much or more about his/her wishes and feelings than what is actually said. Obviously, the lower the age and maturity of the child, the more this is likely to be the case. Euan Ross makes the further point that touch and even smell are additional media which may be important, not only in the particular business of communicating with the child but also in relation to the more general context. Thus, 'the listening person must seem right, look right, smell right'!

Banks (1994), who specializes in work with the younger child, also stresses that 'you need to have more in your kit than just talking'. She uses a wide range of materials and media, including paints and puppets, to facilitate communication.

## The Child Provides Vital Information

Banks (*op cit*), working in a social services context, stresses that it is important to 'understand how the child perceives the situation'. This is a theme which is echoed by all of the chapter authors and by most other commentators, too (e.g. Armstrong, Galloway and Tomlinson, 1993; Cooper, 1993a). The child after all can provide — given the chance — unique, often vital, information about the matters under consideration. Sometimes this may be of an objective nature, where the child as an informant can provide data which no one else is in a position to do. However, often more significantly, the child's own version or understanding of the situation, even where it seems to be at variance with what may be an objective or balanced appraisal, is often an essential starting point for effective communication. This, of course, is equally true for adults.

A 19th century French physician is said to have always taught his paediatric students, 'Listen to the mother: she is giving you the diagnosis'. In the context of our present topic, he might have said: 'Listen to the child: he or she may hold a key to your understanding of the problem — and to its resolution'.

To move from the clinical to the educational setting, the work of Tisdall and Dawson (1994) makes a somewhat similar point. They interviewed twenty-one students who attended a mainstream support facility because of their physical disabilities or hearing impairment. The interviews were designed to elicit the students' views about the education they experienced each day. A number of general conclusions were drawn from the study but what emerged most strongly was the individual, unique responses of the young people involved to what was — objectively — the same set of situations in school.

## Getting the Institutional Framework Right

Thus far, we have largely been concerned to examine factors which the individual professional should have in mind when listening to children. However, the individual does not work in a vacuum and it is essential to consider the framework in which he or she operates. The formal procedures are perhaps a useful starting point, although Peter Smith's chapter reminds us that these are no guarantee that appropriate practice will follow. Training, regular appraisal and monitoring are vital to ensure that the right attitudes and approaches are assimilated into the daily work of each member of a team or service.

Further, senior managers should ensure that the practice of involving children in decision-making and in taking seriously what they say becomes part of the fabric of the institution's ethos and functioning. In a school setting, for example, a school council may be a important way of listening to pupils' views. However:

> School councils are not the only, nor necessarily the best, way of achieving this. Tutorial lessons and House meetings, for example, can also be used for this purpose and questionnaires, especially if they are constructed in consultation with pupils, can be particularly valuable. The view of schools who have used these and other methods to tap the views of pupils is that the responses are on the whole frank, honest, perceptive and useful. (Davie, 1989, p.126; see also Bennathan, 1996, for examples and analyses of good school practice in this respect.)

Irvine Gersch in his chapter, and in many previous publications, identifies another way forward which facilitates the process of institutionalizing the consideration of children's perspectives. Thus, he has developed over a number of years a 'student report', which is completed by the children themselves and which has become an essential feature of the assessments undertaken in his Educational Psychological Service. A somewhat similar approach has been developed by the Surrey Educational Psychology Service (Morton, 1994), which has produced three age-specific reports ('My Learning Report') to be used in schools to elicit pupils' views on their learning — in the context of the Code of Practice, referred to earlier.

The theme of getting the institutional framework right is picked up, too, in Philippa Russell's chapter — in several contexts. Thus, she quotes the experience of Sonia, who has spina bifida and was embarrassed by her mainstream's school's handling of her incontinence problem. Russell comments that the circumstances in which this situation (needlessly) arose are 'a salutary reminder of involving young people in planning as well as assessment and the need to look holistically at the school environment to ensure it is accessible and user-friendly'.

Switching to institutional measures which can be taken at a local authority level, Philippa Russell commends the consideration of advocates for children, which can be a useful device not only in individual cases but also in enhancing the general level of awareness of officers and members. She points to the appointment of children's rights officers in a number of authorities and in one authority an education liaison officer — a joint appointment between education and social services.

## The Voice of the Child as an Agent of Change

As we have seen above, no matter how much the principle of listening to children's wishes and feelings is accepted and even where institutional procedures are modified accordingly, there is often a problem of promoting and consolidating change in individuals and in the service as a whole. Of course, promoting listening to children is no different in this respect from any other change process. Institutions like schools and hospitals have an inbuilt resistance to change. Such resistance does have survival value, in that without it the institution could be jumping on to every passing 'band-wagon' of professional fashion with potentially disastrous results for its stability and continuity. However, occasions arise when this resistance has to be overcome and we have made reference above to some ways forward on this front.

In this context it is interesting to note some evidence to indicate that the practice of consulting children may itself be self-reinforcing and self-validating. This possibility has thus far received little attention in the literature. In essence the suggestion is — in simple terms — that adults who are brought, perhaps reluctantly, to the point of consulting children are often so impressed by children's responses that there is an irreversible conversion to the practice.

Numerous examples of this phenomenon came from an in-service course for senior managers in secondary schools in South-east Wales which focused on learning difficulties and behaviour problems. As an essential part of the course, the teachers were required to seek the views of their pupils about the nature and extent of any aspect of this topic. After much initial scepticism, the course members:

> . . . were often astounded by the balanced views which emerged. One of the headteachers on the course chose to carry out this exercise with a small (but 'difficult') class over several weeks, using a questionnaire that he and the pupils devised together. This very experienced headteacher reported later not only that the information was valuable but that his relationship with the class had been 'transformed' by the experience. (Davie and Galloway, 1996)

Vulliamy and Webb (1991) reported a similar finding in their research which was directed at the identification of factors which appeared to facilitate the change process for teachers undertaking school-based enquiries in the context of their post-graduate training or professional development. One of the major findings of the research was a change in the teachers' attitudes and practice in respect of the increased value they placed on the views of their pupils.

One final example of this phenomenon — more tenuous because the author of the research does not claim it as an example — is nevertheless worth mentioning because of the above findings. The purpose of the enquiry (Francis, 1993) was to encourage trainee teachers to listen carefully to their pupils as the pupils were engaged in learning tasks and to get a better view of them as 'social and personal selves'. Francis found that the trainees' perceptions of their pupils changed positively as a result of this approach and furthermore the pupils' learning improved. Unfortunately, the time frame of the research did not permit Francis to collect evidence as to whether this approach on the part of the trainees persisted — although some of the teachers reported later that it did. Clearly, long-term follow-up of this possible effect would be valuable.


## An Advancing Trend


As this brief review has illustrated, listening to children's wishes and feelings is an advancing trend. The signs of this advance are clear to see in legislation on child law and in the criminal justice system.

The trend has been gathering force in the social services field for a longer period. In fact, it has been suggested elsewhere (Davie, 1993) that the genesis of this trend in social services was a small publication by the National Children's Bureau in 1977, entitled *Who Cares? Children in Care Speak Out* (Page and Clark, 1977). However, even if this explanation is correct, it still leaves open the question as to why this book had the impact that it clearly did. The time was obviously right but perhaps we must leave the social historians to unravel the threads of this event and to put forward a considered analysis in due course.

The remaining two major services for children — education and health — have been slower to 'come on board' but the former, driven in part by the Code of Practice on special educational needs, is now beginning to move. Perhaps this movement is also in part driven by an increasing readiness on the part of schools to recognize the 'consumer' in the system. United Kingdom government policies in recent years have forced this re-orientation. The result has been the growth of a partnership with parents which has characterized the past decade or more.

The child is of course the ultimate consumer in the education system. Therefore, it may be that the acceptance of partnership with parents has in some measure paved the way to the concept of partnership with children and that this will characterize the turn of the century and beyond. Cooper's writings (1993a and 1993b; Cooper and McIntyre, 1993) certainly have some of this ring about them in places. For example, he introduces one of his papers (1993a, p.129), as follows:

> As clients of special educational services pupils are a vital source of information about the nature, quality and effects of the services they receive. Although this article focuses on a study of pupils' perspectives on residential schools for children with emotional and behavioural difficulties, it deals with questions that are important to all those concerned with the nature and quality of SEN provision for pupils. Three questions are asked:

1   Why should we be interested in pupil perspective?
2   How can we get access to the pupil perspective?
3   What can we learn from the pupil perspective?

Whatever the outcome of future analysis as to the reasons for education moving in this direction, there can be little doubt about the movement itself. If further evidence is needed the titles of the following articles taken at random from the Times Educational Supplement make the point:

'The Voice of the Pupil is Heard' (14.1.94., p.10)
'Where Children Write the Rules' (21.1.94., p.13)
'The Importance of Being Listened to' (9.6.95., p.26)

However, there is some way to go yet. As we have seen, child psychiatrists in the UK are part of the process of involving children in decision-making because of the impact of the 1989 Children Act, although not all child psychiatrists are happy at the way this is working out (e.g. Wolkind, *op cit*). Paediatricians, too, are necessarily brought into the process because of the legislation and its effect on child protection procedures. Nevertheless, there is less evidence that the voice of the child is being sought or heeded in family practice or in paediatric clinics. As Euan Ross makes clear there are barriers in the way. He reminds us in his chapter:

Usually it is a joy to listen to children but not always. It can be exhausting. Often a great deal of time is needed before a child can unburden his/her mind to you.

Time is a scarce resource in busy health clinics — no less so in overcrowded classrooms or family centres, of course. Whilst we would be foolish to under-estimate the importance of this factor, some way forward on this front must be found.

One positive aspect of the 'market forces' framework in which most of our services are having now to operate is that it sometimes forces a costing of agreed priorities. Now that the principle is accepted that a child needing special care has a 'right to be heard', and that that practice is also extremely effective in improving the nature and quality of provision, it may be that progress will come more quickly than one might have dared to hope.

### References

ARMSTRONG, D., GALLOWAY, D. and TOMLINSON, S. (1993) 'Assessing special educational needs: the child's contribution', *British Educational Research Journal*, **19**, 2, pp.121–31.
BANKS, S. (1994) 'Giving the young child a voice', *Children Act News*, December, 6.

BENNATHAM, M. (1996) 'Listening to children in schools: An empirical study', in DAVIE, R. and GALLOWAY, D. (Eds) *Listening to Children in Education*, London, David Fulton.

COOPER, P. (1993a) 'Learning from pupil's perspectives', *British Journal of Special Education*, **20**, 4, pp.129–33.

COOPER, P. (1993b) 'Exploring pupils' perceptions of the effects of residential schooling on children with emotional and behavioural difficulties', *Child and Youth Care Forum*, **22**, 2, pp.125–41.

COOPER, P. and McINTYRE, D. (1993) 'Commonality in teachers' and pupils' perceptions of effective classroom learning', *British Journal of Educational Psychology*, **63**, pp.381–99.

DAVIE, R. (1993) 'Listen to the child: a time for change', *The Psychologist*, **6**, 6, pp.252–57.

DAVIE, R. (1994) 'A consortium for children: analysis of the dialogue with policymakers leading to the 1993 Education Act and the 1994 Code of Practice', *Therapeutic Care and Education*, **3**, 3, pp.206–17.

DAVIE, R. and GALLOWAY, D. (1996) 'The voice of the child in education', in DAVIE, R. and GALLOWAY, D. (Eds) *Listening to Children in Education*, London, David Fulton.

DEPARTMENT FOR EDUCATION (1994) *Code of Practice on the Identification and Assessment of Special Educational Needs*, London, DFE.

FRANCIS, H. (1993) *Teachers Listening to Learners' Voices*, British Psychological Society Education Section, Leicester, BPS.

FREEMAN, M. (1996) 'Children's education: a test case for best interest and autonomy', in DAVIE, R. and GALLOWAY, D. (Eds) *Listening to Children in Education*, London, David Fulton.

GILLICK (1985) *Gillick v West Norfolk and Wisbech Area Health Authority and Department of Health and Social Security*, 3 AER 402.

HENDRICK, H. (1992) 'Children and childhood, *ReFRESH*', 15, Autumn.

MORTON, J. (1994) *Involving the Child: Code of Practice School-Based Assessment. Teachers Pack*, Kingston-upon-Thames, Surrey CC.

NEWELL, P. (1988) 'Children's rights after Cleveland', *Children and Society*, 3, pp.199–206.

PAGE, R. and CLARKE, G.A. (1977) (Eds) *Who Cares? Children in Care Speak Out*, London, NCB.

SPENCER, J. (1990a) *The Evidence of Children — the Law and the Psychology*, London, Blackburn Press.

SPENCER, P. (1990b) 'Persuading the courts to listen to children', in BANNISTER, A., BARRETT, K. and SHEARER, E. (Eds) *Listening to Children*, London, Longman.

THE TIMES (1992) 'Tell me off and I'll phone my lawyer', *The Times Newspaper*, November 17, 33.

TIMES EDUCATIONAL SUPPLEMENT (1994) 'The voice of the child is heard', 14 January, 10.

TIMES EDUCATIONAL SUPPLEMENT (1994) 'Where children write the rules', 21 January, 13.

TIMES EDUCATIONAL SUPPLEMENT (1995) 'The importance of being listened to', 9 June, 26.

TISDALL, G. and DAWSON, R. (1994) 'Listening to children: interviews with children attending a mainstream support facility', *Support for Learning*, **9**, 4, pp.179–82.

VULLIAMY, G. and WEBB, R. (1991) 'Teacher research and educational change: an empirical study', *British Educational Research Journal*, **17**, 3, pp.219–36.

WADE, B. and MOORE, M. (1993) *Experiencing Special Education*, Milton Keynes, Open University Press.

WOLKIND, S. (1993) 'The 1989 Children Act: a cynical view from an ivory tower', *Association for Child Psychology and Psychiatry Newsletter*, **15**, 1, pp.40–1.

*Part I*

*Professional Perspectives*

# 1 The Law in Relation to the Wishes and Feelings of the Child

*Michael Sherwin*

The Children Act 1989, which came into force on 14 October 1991, was the product of a great deal of thought and research, and brought about the most fundamental change of child law this century. There is frequent reference to the wishes and feelings of the child involved in civil proceedings. All parents are familiar with the difference between what a child wants and what is in its best interests; the legislators recognize this too but it is not always easy either for legislators or for those entrusted to make decisions on behalf of children to get the balance between the two right. This chapter will attempt to set out the ways in which the voice of the child may be heard in legal proceedings today. It is not offered as a comprehensive analysis; that would be impossible within the available space, in an inter-disciplinary text, but it is hoped that the points made in this chapter will be of assistance to professionals of other disciplines in putting particular problems in a legal context.

In Victorian times, children were said to be 'seen and not heard'. At the time of the Supreme Court Act 1873 children were regarded by the law, along with married women and lunatics, as 'persons under disability', unable to bring or defend legal proceedings without a 'next friend' or 'guardian ad litem.' The thought that they might have a voice in legal proceedings concerning their future was unheard of.

The legal position of married women improved as society developed in a less paternalistic way, as to some extent did the position of mentally handicapped persons as society became more sensitive, but the position of children was quite slow to change. By 1970 there were two main ways in which children could come into the compulsory care of a local authority — by the local authority assuming parental rights, in respect of children in their voluntary care (Children Act 1948, S2) or by application to the court for a care order under Section 1 of the Children and Young Persons Act 1969. I do not propose to discuss children being remanded into care by a criminal court since this chapter is primarily concerned with the child's voice in civil proceedings.

Parental rights resolutions could be challenged by the parents; the contest in court was between the local authority and the parents and the voice of the child was not separately heard.

Under the 1969 Act, a solicitor was appointed to represent the child; the parents could be represented but legal aid was not available for them. On the whole the child's solicitor tended to represent the views of the parents. Applications to discharge care orders were contests between the parents and the local authority.

In November 1971 a juvenile court granted an application to discharge a seven year old child named Maria Colwell from care. Fourteen months later she was battered to death by her stepfather. From the report of the subsequent enquiry[1] came the involvement in such cases of an independent guardian ad litem to investigate the circumstances and prepare a report with recommendations based on the child's needs, wishes and feelings.

The practice then developed whereby in most public law proceedings concerning children, the court would appoint a guardian ad litem to represent the child. The court would often appoint the child's solicitor. The court rules were amended in 1984, enabling parents to be full parties to care proceedings, which meant that they could have their own representation if necessary paid for by the legal aid fund, and the influence of guardians ad litem meant that solicitors gradually began to recognize that the interests of the child may be different from those of the parents.

There were many cases concerning children which required a more flexible approach than was available under the Children Act 1948 (by then the Child Care Act 1980) or the Children and Young Persons Act 1969 (for example until 1984 parents had no right to challenge a decision by a local authority to refuse them access to a child in their care), and in the 1980s local authorities and to a lesser extent, family members resorted increasingly to the ancient *parens patriae* jurisdiction of the High Court by having a child made a ward of court.

The Official Solicitor to the Supreme Court, an office which has existed since 1876 to represent the interests of litigants not able to represent themselves, found himself increasingly being asked by the court to represent the interests of the children who were the subject of wardship proceedings. The Official Solicitor regarded his function as representing to the court a solution which he considered to be in the child's best interests.

The Law Society decided in 1986 to establish a panel of solicitors approved by the Society as being competent to represent children in legal proceedings. Admission to the Child Care Panel (now the Children Panel) was by proven experience and demonstration of knowledge of the law, procedure and need to handle such cases with sensitivity.

Despite all these improvements cases continued to occur throughout the 1980s of children killed despite the involvement of the welfare services and the reports into these deaths, together with the Cleveland Report[2] contributed much to the thought which was to go into the Children Act 1989.

Under the Children Act 1989 the courts apply uniform principles when dealing with private and public law cases concerning children. Private law cases are cases between two or more individuals concerning a child. Public law cases are cases in which the State in the form of a local authority or the NSPCC is a party. How is the voice of the child heard?

Fundamentally, the court is enjoined by Section 1(1) to regard the child's welfare as its paramount consideration when it determines any question with respect to the upbringing of a child or the administration of a child's property. The court is given guidance, when dealing with a public law case or a disputed private law case, in what has become known as the 'welfare check list' in Section 1(3) which requires the court to have regard in particular to —

(a) The ascertainable wishes and feelings of the child concerned (considered in the light of his (sic) age and understanding);

(b) his physical, emotional and educational needs;

(c) the likely effect on him of any change in his circumstances;

(d) his age, sex, background, and any characteristics of his which the court considers relevant;

(e) any harm which he has suffered or is at risk of suffering;

(f) How capable each of his parents, and any other person in relation to whom the court considers the question to be relevant, is of meeting his needs;

(g) the range of powers available to the court under this Act in the proceedings in question.

Similarly, when a child is being looked after by a local authority (whether accommodated or subject to a care order), the local authority is under a duty, before making any decision with respect to a child, so far as is reasonably practicable to ascertain the wishes and feelings of (among others) the child regarding the matter to be decided (Section 22(4)) and, in making any decision, to give due consideration (having regard to age and understanding) to the child's wishes and feelings, and to the child's religious persuasion, racial origin and cultural and linguistic background (Section 22(5)).

Section 26 enables the Secretary of State to make regulations requiring the case of each child looked after by a local authority to be reviewed periodically. The regulations may make provision requiring the authority, before conducting any review, to seek the views of (among others) the child, to notify the child of the result of the review and to establish a complaints procedure which enables the child, among others, to make representations. Thus, the statutory complaints procedure provides a means whereby the older child can try to affect change in the way a local authority proposes to discharge its obligations towards him or her.

These statutory obligations and attendant regulations are designed to ensure that the local authority who is looking after a child does not lose sight of the wishes and feelings of that child, and the legislators expected that they would have a powerful impact on the way local authorities discharge their responsibilities.

In practice, a child is not in a powerful position because it takes enormous courage to complain about the care system from within it. The independent element is only a small part of the complaints procedure, and the legislation is worded in such a way as to give local authorities a great deal of discretion as to the use of resources. The child's only remedy after rejection of a complaint under Section 26 is an application to the High Court for a judicial review, a procedure fraught with technical difficulty.

The local authority's obligations probably have most impact when the child is the subject of a public law application. Whilst the proceedings are pending the court exercises control over the matter. Its leave is required before a child undergoes a medical or psychiatric examination where the results of that examination are to be used in evidence in the proceedings. It expects the local authority to put forward a detailed care plan for the child which can, where necessary, be criticized by other parties to the proceedings.

The child's protection does not, however, extend as far as allowing children to claim damages in respect of breach of the statutory duties imposed on local authorities and others under the Children Act 1989 or its predecessors, nor does any action lie in negligence in respect of a local authority's failure to exercise its statutory duties. These points were established by two cases decided in 1994.[3] In one of these, the *Bedfordshire case*, the Court dismissed a claim by five children against their local authority for damages for breach of duty arising from an alleged series of failures in the discharge of the authority's statutory functions under the relevant child care legislation, resulting in personal injury to themselves; in the *Newham case* the child unsuccessfully sought to claim damages against the local authority in whose care she had spent almost one year on the basis of allegations, which turned out to be unsubstantiated, that she had been sexually abused. The House of Lords has upheld the Court of Appeal's decisions (*The Times*, Law Report, 1995, June 30).

The voice of the child will be specifically heard in public law cases under the Children Act 1989, since by Section 41 the court is obliged in such proceedings to appoint a guardian ad litem for the child unless satisfied that it is not necessary to do so in order to safeguard his or her interests. One of the guardian ad litem's duties is to appoint a solicitor to represent the child (although in some areas the solicitor's appointment is still made by the court); in either case the child's solicitor will be a member of the Law Society's Children Panel. Thus the child will have a formidable team concerned to safeguard his or her interests in the proceedings, with one professional carrying out most of the investigation and the other putting forward the child's case in court, and the two working together in partnership.[4] A guardian ad litem is entitled to examine and copy the local authority's records and have them admitted into evidence in the proceedings (Section 42).

The Act, however, has thrown up one or two anomalies; for example, there is no provision for the appointment of a guardian ad litem for proceedings concerning an education supervision order, even though the child's interest are paramount and the welfare checklist applies; on the other hand a guardian is likely to be appointed in proceedings for a child to be kept in secure accommodation although in such proceedings the child's welfare is not paramount.

Free legal aid is now automatically available to children, and to parents with parental responsibility, for applications for care or supervision orders (although means and merit tests are applied on applications for contact with the child in care or application to discharge a child from care).

Problems can arise when an older child takes a view of the case different from its guardian ad litem. From whom does the solicitor take instructions? The solicitor's professional rules are quite clear — if the child is old enough to give the solicitor instructions, the solicitor must act on those instructions, and in court he must act as advocate for the child client's case. This leaves the guardian ad litem unrepresented by an advocate unless the local authority agrees to pay.

The position of the child's voice in private law proceedings is less straightforward. The child is not, as in public law proceedings, automatically made a party to the proceedings. The duty to appoint a guardian ad litem unless this is unnecessary (Section 41(1)) is not applicable; one difficulty is that no fund has been established out of which the expenses of a guardian ad litem in private law cases can be paid. In most cases the courts rely on the services of court welfare officers to investigate and report on disputed matters (Section 7).

Before the Children Act 1989 most legislation enabled the court hearing an application concerning a child to make a care order or supervision order to the local authority if, in an exceptional case, that was felt to be appropriate. Since the Children Act 1989 was passed, the criteria in Section 31 provide the only route by which such orders can now be made. If the court hearing a private law case concerning a child (or certain other applications as well) takes the view that it may be appropriate for a care or supervision order to be made with respect to the child, it may direct the appropriate authority to undertake an investigation of the child's circumstances (Section 37). The local authority is obliged, when undertaking the investigation, to consider whether to apply for a care or supervision order in respect of the child, and if they decide not to apply, they must inform the court of their reasons for so deciding. The court has jurisdiction to appoint a guardian ad litem when directing a local authority to undertake an investigation, and is likely to do so if it feels that an interim order should be made there and then[5] and the court will review the matter in the light of the local authority's investigation. The investigation may or may not result in an application by the local authority for a care or supervision order.

The weakness of Section 37 is that if the local authority, having investigated, decide not to make an application, there is nothing the court can do. This was starkly illustrated in a case[6] in which the issue was whether the court could make orders excluding the father from the family home, he having sexually abused one or more of the children; the local authority applied for an order excluding the father; the judge held that he had no jurisdiction to make such an order on the application of the local authority although that result could have been achieved had the local authority applied for a care order. The Court of Appeal expressed itself thus:

The court is deeply concerned at the absence of any power to direct this authority to take steps to protect the children. In the former wardship jurisdiction it might well have been able to do so. The operation of the Children Act 1989 is entirely dependent on the full co-operation of all those involved. This includes the courts, local authorities, social workers, and all who have to deal with children. Unfortunately, as it appears from this case, if a local authority doggedly resists taking the steps which are appropriate to the case of children at risk of suffering significant harm, it appears that the court is powerless. The authority may perhaps lay itself open to an application for judicial review, but in a case such as this the question arises, at whose instance? The position is one which it is to be hoped will not recur.

It is rare for the court to order that children should be separately represented in proceedings between their parents. In one case[7] the Court of Appeal decided that the children who were involved in a matrimonial dispute about contact should be made parties to the proceedings and be separately represented by a solicitor who at the same time acted as the children's guardian ad litem. The welfare officer had told the court that she could not adequately present the children's views to the court, which the Court of Appeal regarded as very significant; the Court of Appeal upheld the judge's view that the children should be separately represented because of a foreign element (both parents were Australian; the father wanted to return to Australia; the mother wanted to stay in England), the potential conflict of loyalties, the possibility of pressure on the children, and the overall need to ascertain what the children genuinely felt about their future in a difficult situation. The Court of Appeal added that the father was a dominant personality and that the children were unable to convince him that their contact with the mother was inadequate.

To what extent the courts follow this decision and allow separate representation for children in private law cases remains to be seen.

The Children Act came into force accompanied by detailed regulations, rules of court and guidance published by the Department of Health. Of concern to some commentators was the lack of ways in which the child could bring an unsatisfactory situation to the attention of the court. Although it is clear from the way Section 10 is drafted that a child can, with the leave of the court, make its own application for a residence, contact, specific issue or prohibited steps order (by Section 10(8), the court may only grant leave if satisfied that the child has sufficient understanding to make the proposed application) a child is still regarded by the law as under a disability and therefore would need a 'next friend' to make the application. In the nature of the situation, a parent is unlikely to be a suitable 'next friend' so how is the child to put an application before the court?

The court rules were amended with effect from 1st April 1992[8] to allow a child to begin, pursue or defend private law proceedings without a next friend or guardian ad litem if he has obtained the leave of the court, or where a solicitor has accepted the child's instructions to act and considers that the child is able, having regard to his or her understanding, to give instructions in relation to the proceedings. The amended rules were considered by the Court of Appeal in two cases in the early part of 1993.[9] In re S the Court of Appeal upheld a judge's decision to refuse an application by an 11 year old boy to conduct legal proceedings without his guardian ad litem, the Official Solicitor. The court held that the real issue was whether the child had sufficient understanding to give coherent instructions. It was understanding, not age, which was important. The court said that the Children Act 1989 required a judicious balance to be struck between two considerations; that children were human beings in their own right with individual minds and wills, views, and emotions, which should command serious attention, and that a child was, after all, a child.

In re CT the appeal concerned the rights of a child aged 13 to initiate family proceedings against her parents without the intervention of a next friend. The Court of Appeal, allowing her to do so, made it clear that the court, rather than the solicitor, has the ultimate right to decide whether a child who comes before it as a party without a next friend or guardian ad litem has the necessary ability, having regard to her understanding, to instruct her solicitor.

The amendment to the rules does not solve all the problems, however. The effect of the amendment is to give a child full party status, with access to all reports and statements filed with the court, the right to cross examine and the obligation to submit himself for cross-examination by other parties. The Court of Appeal is clearly troubled by the implications of a child making his or her own application. Judges are even anxious about children of 13 years of age sitting in court throughout the hearing of an appeal against the making of a care order. In re C[10] the child had been present in court throughout the hearing before the magistrates and also throughout the appeal hearing. She had expressly asked to be present and her guardian ad litem felt strongly that she would benefit from the experience. The judge said that if guardians ad litem were proposing to arrange for children as young as this to be present at an appeal, they should give that question very careful consideration and be prepared to explain their reasons to the judge.

There have been some cases of this kind highlighted in the popular press where children have made their own applications for residence orders, e.g. to be allowed to live with an aunt, a birth parent (despite having been adopted) or the parents of a boyfriend. The President of the Family Division, recognizing the sensitivity of such cases, has directed that children's applications for leave must be dealt with by a High Court Judge. We do not appear quite to have reached the position as in parts of the USA where a child was apparently allowed to 'divorce' her parents.

There are other kinds of legal proceedings in which the child's future may be at stake. In an adoption application the child is not a party to the proceedings unless the case is brought in the High Court. This seems illogical and there is much to be said for making the child a party and giving the court discretion to allow separate representation. In non-agreed cases the court is likely to appoint a guardian ad litem who will report to the court on the wishes and feelings, as well as the needs, of the child. In the High Court the child will have representation even in the simplest case.

Section 6 of the Adoption Act 1976 requires the court, in reaching any decision relating to the adoption of a child, to have regard to all the circumstances, first consideration being given to the need to safeguard and promote the child's welfare throughout his or her childhood. The court shall so far as is practicable ascertain the wishes and feelings of the child regarding the decision and give due consideration to them, having regard to the child's age and understanding.

It is likely that a new Adoption Act will appear on the statute books in the next few years. One of the proposals in the government's Adoption Law Review is that no child of 12 or older should be adopted unless that child specifically agrees. This proposal, mirrored in adoption legislation in Scotland and some of the American states, seems peculiar as one cannot readily imagine a court granting an adoption order in respect of an older child who did not wish to be adopted, or remaining in ignorance of such a child's wishes and feelings.

Child abduction cases are essentially disputes between the abducting and victim parents. The child is not normally a party. The UK is a signatory to the Hague Convention on International Child Abduction:[11] The relevant legislation — the Child Abduction and Custody Act 1985 — provides for a summary means whereby the court can order the child's return to the country from which it was abducted. The application for return can be resisted if the court is satisfied that there is a grave risk that his or her return would expose the child to physical or psychological harm or otherwise place the child in an intolerable situation (Article 13). Return may be refused if it is found that the child objects to being returned and has attained an age and degree of maturity at which it is appropriate to take account of its views. The court's normal practice where this is raised as an issue is to invite a court welfare officer to interview the child and report to the court.

Two Convention cases decided within a month of one another in the Court of Appeal illustrate the court's thinking on hearing the voice of the child. In each case the leading judgment was given by Lord Justice Butler-Sloss. In the first case,[12] decided on 22nd November 1993, the judge had made a consent order that two boys aged 11 and nearly 10 be returned to Australia forthwith. The mother decided not to return with them. Both boys were upset and when they embarked on the plane the elder boy 'created a scene of a nature which caused the pilot to refuse to fly with him on board'. The two boys were returned to the mother pending her appeal against the consent order. The Court of Appeal allowed the appeal against the order for the boys' return to Australia, but upheld the judge's decision to refuse to join the children as parties to the proceedings holding that the court welfare officer was the 'obvious person' to inform the court of the boys' views.

In the second case,[13] decided on 21st December 1993, the Court of Appeal upheld the judge's decision joining a 13 year old boy as a party to a Convention application, holding that although a child should only be made a party to such an application in exceptional cases, the present case, where the dispute was between mother and child, not mother and father, and where the only effective way for the boys' objections to return to Ireland to be considered by the court was by his own legal representation, was such a case. The boy had repeatedly run away from the home in Ireland of his mother and her partner, alleging violence by the partner, and the mother had pursued a course of relentless litigation in order to establish control of the boy and was seeking ultimately to have him confined in a secure unit.

The most difficult cases have concerned the child expressing a wish to refuse medical treatment to sustain life — in effect expressing a wish to die. In June 1994 a 15 year old boy in Florida persuaded a judge there to let him return home from hospital to which he had been taken against his will when he stopped taking what were described as painful and debilitating drugs. The judge acknowledged the boy's right to make his own decision; the boy was reported as saying that he knew the problems and consequences.

The law in the UK has not gone that far. Since 1969 a child aged 16 or over has been able to give consent to any surgical, medical or dental treatment; the doctors are not obliged to seek consent from the child's parents.[14] This provision does not, however, mean that children under the age of 16 can never give a valid consent. In 1982 Mrs Gillick went to court to challenge guidance issued by the relevant government department which suggested that doctors may prescribe contraceptive pills to girls under the age of 16 without seeking parental consent. The challenge was unsuccessful; the House of Lords held that provided that they are of sufficient age and understanding, children under the age of 16 can give valid consent. The case gave rise to the expression 'Gillick competent', meaning that a child under the age of 16 may give valid consent if the child understands the nature of the advice being given, and is of sufficient maturity to understand what is involved.[15]

In the later case of re R[16] it was argued that a 'Gillick competent child' could also veto any proposed treatment. The child was in a psychiatric hospital and could only be treated with the use of drugs which she refused to accept. The local authority made the child a Ward of Court and the question was whether the court would have the power to override the child's veto. The Court of Appeal held that all that the Gillick case decided was that a competent child could give a valid consent, not that such a child could withhold consent. This seems to be a clear example of the court listening to the child's wishes and feelings but overriding them.

In a later case[17] the court held that it could override both a 16 year old and a 'Gillick competent' child's refusal to consent to treatment. The case concerned a 16 year old girl whose parents had died of cancer when she was very young; she was taken into care and her foster placements were disastrous and resulted in her being referred to a clinic, suffering from depression and a nervous tic. Symptoms of anorexia nervosa manifested themselves and when she was almost 15 she was in need of in-patient treatment in a specialist residential home. While there she displayed violence towards the staff and began to injure herself until she reached a stage when she had to be fed by nasogastric tube and have her arms encased in plaster. Against that background the local authority applied to the court to give her medical treatment without her consent. The child was represented by the Official Solicitor. The Court of Appeal decided that the court should approach the exercise of discretion with a predilection to give effect to the child's wishes on the basis that prima facie it would be in her best interests; however, it was known that anorexia was capable of destroying the ability to make an informed choice and when the case came to court, the child's condition had deteriorated so drastically that the court would have been in dereliction of its duty had it not overridden her wishes and given the local authority the authority to give her medical treatment.

Parliament's approach to the problem in the child protection part of the Children Act 1989 is to give a 'Gillick competent' child the right to refuse to submit to medical or psychiatric examination. Such a provision is to be found in Section 43 (Child Assessment Order) Section 44 (Emergency Protection Order) and Section 38 (Interim Care or Supervision Orders). Possibly in this area Parliament adopts a more permissive approach (respecting the wishes and feelings of a 'Gillick competent' child) than the courts, who adopt a paternalistic approach (we shall if we think it best overrule the child's wishes).

Clearly this is a very sensitive area. Adults entrusted with responsibility for making decisions about children will want to act as wise parents. Part of a child's development must include learning to exercise freedom of choice, which can involve exercising freedom to make mistakes. A parent can only offer guidance. In certain extreme situations, however, such as self destruction or self-harm, the courts will intervene.

The law concerning children underwent a fundamental change with the implementation of the Children Act 1989 on 14th October 1991. In the ensuing three and a half years a body of case law has developed our understanding of the Act and many matters have been clarified by the higher courts. Two cases have gone on appeal to the House of Lords and it was interesting that in one of them, concerning the threshold criteria, the Judicial Committee was chaired by the Lord Chancellor who overturned a narrow construction placed upon the relevant section by the Court of Appeal. Clearly those at the top of our judicial system wish to see the Act working with the degree of flexibility which Parliament intended.

The judges of the Family Division of the High Court have an integral role to play in the implementation of the Act, since they hear the most serious cases at first instance, and also hear appeals from decisions of the magistrates. They have had much to say about the quality of magistrates' reasons for their decisions and about the proper approach to justify state intervention in the life of a child, and the contact a child should have with members of its family after it comes into care, and with the parent with whom it is not living. The judges are clearly concerned with delays in achieving decisions for children and have become much more closely involved in the management of cases than before, insisting upon tighter control of expert evidence, orderly presentation of documents, narrowing down of issues in dispute and the time taken for substantive hearings — such judicial intervention is not part of British judicial tradition but is prompted by the need for more efficient management of court time as well as the need for more expeditious handling of litigation.

So far as the voice of the child is concerned, the philosophy of the Act is clearly tempered by a degree of judicial paternalism derived possibly from the experience of the judges (both as judges and as advocates) from the days of wardship proceedings and there is a clear recognition that cases concerning children which come to court require the same forensic skills and critical analysis of the evidence as other cases, despite the greater flexibility and less strict approach to the calling of evidence which necessarily obtains in cases concerning children. The courts will always seek to achieve what is in the child's best interests and ultimately the question what is in the child's best interests must be a matter for judicial decision.

The purpose of the present chapter has been to discuss how the child's voice in civil proceedings can be heard to contribute to the court's decision. There are nowadays far more safeguards and better procedures than in the past to ensure that the child's voice is heard. In the end, however, we have to remember that in proceedings under the Children Act 1989 it is the child's welfare, not wishes and feelings, which is paramount. Responsibility for decisions concerning children has to be taken by adults.

### Notes

1 Report of the Committee of Inquiry into the Care and Supervision Provided in Relation to Maria Colwell (DHSS).
2 Report of the Inquiry into Child Abuse in Cleveland (Cmd 412, 1988).
3 X and others -v- Bedfordshire County Council and M and others -v- London Borough of Newham (1994) 1 FLR 431.
4 'Speaking out for Children', published by the Children's Society 1990.
5 Judgment of Mr Justice Wall in re CE ( A minor) (1995) FLR 26.
6 Nottinghamshire County Council -v- P (1993) 2 FLR 134.
7 L -v- L (Minor: Separate Representation) (1994) 1 FLR 156.
8 Family Proceedings Rules 1991, amended by SI 1992/456.
9 Re S (A minor) (Independent Representation) (1993) 2 FLR 437; Re CT (A minor) (Wardship: Representation) (1993) 2 FLR 278.
10 Re C (A minor) (Care: child's wishes) (1993) 1 FLR 832.
11 The Convention on the Civil Aspects of International Child Abduction, signed at The Hague on 25th October 1980.
12 Re M (minors) (Child Abduction) (1994) 1 FLR 390.
13 Re M (A minor) (Abduction: Child's Objections) (1994) 2 FLR 126.
14 Family Law Reform Act 1969, Section 8(1).
15 Gillick -v- West Norfolk and Wisbech Area Health Authority and Department of Health and Social Security (1985) 3 AER 402.

16  Re R (A minor) (Wardship: Medical Treatment) (1992) 4 AER 177.
17  Re W (A minor) (Medical Treatment) (1992) 4 AER 627.

## References

WHITE, R.A.H. (1994) *Clarke, Hall and Morrison on Children*, Sevenoaks, Butterworths.
HERSHMAN, D. and MCFARLANE, A. (1994) *Children Law and Practice*, Bristol, Family Law, Jordan Publishing.

Abbreviations:  FLR  =  Family Law Reports
AER  =  All England Law Reports

# 2    Listening to Children in Educational Contexts

*Irvine S. Gersch*
*(with Shirley Moyse, Anna Nolan and Graham Pratt)*

This chapter examines the educational context within which children's views are sought. It discusses some recent legislative and attitudinal changes in respect of pupil involvement. Several illustrative innovative projects are reviewed including the development of the Student Report and principles for developing such tools are outlined. Some complex issues, dilemmas and concerns facing professionals and parents working in this area are highlighted and explored and a checklist, with a view to increasing pupil involvement in assessment and school life, for (a) schools and teachers, (b) LEAs and (c) other professionals offered. Finally, the chapter concludes with some general comments about the trends in this area, and indicates some broad areas for future development.

It is the underlying thesis of this chapter that the principles and philosophy of pupil involvement are more important than the actual techniques, and that there are many different and valuable ways of working in this area. Indeed, schools, parents, LEAs, teachers and other professionals will all inevitably be at different points in respect of the continuum of pupil involvement.

## The Educational Context

During recent years there has been a growing interest in and acceptance of the value of increasing the active participation of children in decisions made about them and their school life. Children are viewed by many teachers as needing to take an active role as learners, if they are to make effective progress, and for them to be involved in the assessments which are made of their progress and needs. However, the picture is patchy and there is certainly scope for increasing the active involvement of children in all forms of school life (Davie, 1993). In respect of children with special educational needs, there has been a recognition of the imperative to involve children as fully as possible in all aspects of their assessments.

The author has argued elsewhere (Gersch, 1987, 1992) that there are at least three major reasons for involving children in their assessments, including legally supported, moral and pragmatic. From a legal point of view, the statutory

1994 Code of Practice, the Children Act (1989) and indeed United Nations Convention all encourage educational professionals to seek the views of children in assessment and plans made about them. Morally, it can be argued readily that children should be informed and actively engaged in any assessments made about them, and indeed they have a right to be involved all through the process, from understanding what is happening, to giving their point of view, to being provided with their results. Finally, from a purely practical and pragmatic point of view, we do know that all plans are likely to work more successfully and assessments become more reliable and valid where children themselves have a sense of ownership and commitment to the outcomes, which have been negotiated with them.

Two further reasons for seeking pupils' views about their assessments and school plans are:

(a) that the process tends to boost their self confidence and self image and

(b) pupil feedback provides a unique evaluation to assist teachers wishing to improve the effectiveness of their teaching.

It is possible to view the history of pupil involvement as going through several phases. In Victorian times children were meant to be 'seen and not heard', and were regarded as passive objects. In more recent years, the needs of children, as people in their own right, have been re-examined. Indeed, in the legal system, education and society generally, there has been a move to recognizing such rights, as separate from those of their parents and teachers.

Clifford (1993) has argued that children's views have on occasion been afforded a somewhat unrealistic status, as always correct, reliable, valid and worthy of superseding the evidence of adults. In child abuse cases in court, for example, it is possible that certain professionals have tended to support any child's assertion and the 'False Memory Syndrome' phenomenon (which recognizes that children's evidence might be mistaken) has acted as a slight brake to such excesses. Clifford's own experimental evidence demonstrates that children are more prone to error and memory lapses than adults and they are probably more susceptible to unconscious persuasion and influence than adults, too.

In schools, it is likely that there is variable practice, somewhere between the first phase of children being seen and not heard and the second phase of seeking to engage children and consult them about many aspects of school life. However, there are good reasons to believe that pupil involvement is an area of development which is likely to grow significantly within the foreseeable future.

Within education, schools and the area of special educational needs there would appear to be at least six areas on which pupil involvement might impinge, which are as follows:

(i) decision making about the school generally,

(ii) participating in the learning processes, that is, through teacher styles which encourage active student learning,

(iii)   the assessment of individual progress, targets and achievements, strengths and weaknesses,

(iv)   the assessment of special educational needs, aims and targets, individual educational plans, and special educational provisions and arrangements needed.

(v)   pupil choices about courses and extra-curricular activities.

(vi)   pupil choices about which school they attend.

## Recent Legislative and Policy Changes: the Code of Practice

There have been several pieces of legislation and policy which impact directly upon pupil involvement in school, perhaps the most influential being the Children Act (1989) and the 1994 Code of Practice on the identification and assessment of special educational needs, which derives from the 1993 Education Act.

The Children Act 1989 (White *et al.*, 1990) states that when reaching decisions about children, the ascertainable wishes and feelings of the child must be taken into account, consideration being given to the child's age and understanding. The general principle of listening to children, taking their views seriously and giving them due weight is a key element in this Act.

Circular 22/89 relating to the 1981 Education Act, and detailing processes for the assessment of children with special educational needs also indicated that, wherever possible, the views and feelings of the child should be included and taken into account.

More recently, the 1993 Education Act required the Secretary of State to issue a Code of Practice giving guidance to those working with children with special educational needs. From September 1 1994, all those working in the area of special educational needs have to consider what the Code says, and they 'have a statutory duty to have regard to it; they must not ignore it' (p.11). It is worth citing the relevant section of the Code directly given the clear and succinct advice which is offered, since this sets out the most recent thinking for educational professionals working in the area of special educational needs. Sections 2.34 to 2.38 of the Code of Practice (pages 14–15) highlight the importance of involving the child in any assessment and intervention. It states that:

> The effectiveness of any assessment and intervention will be influenced by the involvement and interest of the child and young person concerned. (DFE, p.14)

The Code describes practical benefits for involving children, stating that children have important information to contribute and that their support is crucial for effective planning. The Code also highlights the point that children have a 'right to be heard', in respect of decisions made about them.

The Code goes on to state that:

Schools should, therefore, make every effort to identify the ascertainable views and wishes of the child or young person about his or her current and future education. Positive pupil involvement is unlikely to happen spontaneously. Careful attention, guidance and encouragement will be required to help pupils respond relevantly and fully. Young people are more likely to respond positively to intervention programmes if they fully understand the rationale for their involvement and if they are given some personal responsibility for their own progress. Schools should, for example, discuss the purpose of a particular assessment arrangement with the child; invite comments from the child; and consider the use of pupil reports and systematic feedback to the child concerned. Many children with special educational needs have little self-confidence and low self-esteem. Involving children in tracking their own progress within a programme designed to meet their particular learning or behavioural difficulty can contribute to an improved self image and greater self confidence. (DFE, 1994, pp.14–15)

Finally, it is perhaps worth indicating that such moves toward increased active child involvement are not just a British phenomenon, but have world-wide interest. The United Nations Convention on the Rights of the Child (1989), which was adopted by the UK Government in 1991, and by 1994 had been signed by 175 countries, states that children should be assured the right to express their views freely in all matters affecting them, their views being given due weight in accordance with their age and maturity.

## School Attitudes to Pupil Involvement: A Recent Survey

In order to investigate how far schools and colleges had developed their practice and to obtain a brief snapshot of attitudes about pupil involvement, the author, together with Shirley Moyse carried out a small scale survey of the issue.

The aim of this study was to identify whether schools and colleges valued and therefore wished to encourage pupil involvement, particularly in the central areas of assessment, curriculum and decision making. It also aimed to examine whether, in the light of recent trends and legislation, it was perceived that there had been an increase in pupil involvement during the past ten years. It was hoped that interesting initiatives and examples of good practice would be identified. The project was undertaken in May and June 1994 in an outer London borough. Given the constraints of time, a questionnaire was sent out to all Heads of Nursery, Infant, Junior, Primary, Secondary, Special Schools and Colleges in the area. A total of 87 organizations were contacted. Of these, nearly 40 per cent (33) completed and returned their questionnaires.

The overwhelming majority of respondents indicated that pupil involvement should be encouraged and also felt that to some extent it was being encouraged in their organization. The majority of responses also indicated that it was perceived that there was higher degree of pupil involvement than ten years ago. In the important areas of assessment, curriculum and decision making, once again the majority of organizations which responded felt that pupils were involved to some degree.

It was in the area of assessment where schools indicated greatest pupil involvement and in the area of curriculum least. A number of schools referred to the fact that involvement had now to be set within the framework of the National Curriculum. The findings indicate that assessment in schools is now viewed as more of a partnership between teacher and student. The most commonly reported method of assessing the merits of work, at all ages, was through discussion. Pupils were said to be given opportunities to choose what they believed to be their best piece of work for assessment. In the area of curriculum a large proportion of schools surveyed had implemented reading partnership schemes, such as paired reading. Such schemes typically involve a parent listening to a child read, but taking over the reading when the child indicates that he or she wants this to happen (such as by tapping on the table). The child tends to take an active and leading role in the reading practice.

When it came to decision making, pupils were most often involved in drawing up behaviour policy and school councils were seen as important ways of involving pupils both in secondary and primary schools. The issues discussed at council meetings were often more sophisticated than teachers might have expected and often led to improvements in the school's procedures. Other schemes reported were victim/bully support groups, pupil-run newspapers, pupils selecting their own rewards and involvement in school development plans. In one primary school pupils set rules and modelled acceptable ways of behaving that were then photographed. These photographs formed the basis of a booklet on behaviour which was then sent home to parents. A girls' secondary school outlined their method of choosing prefects, where staff and pupils voted together and that also involved those shortlisted attending a 'leadership' weekend in Wales.

Although the study was constrained by the time available and by the sample size, and perhaps location, it is felt that the findings are of interest in depicting significant developments during the past ten years. However, as a small scale study, with a 38 per cent response rate, cautious interpretation of the findings are in order, since it is possible that our findings were biased in favour of the converted. A number of schools intimated, on their returned questionnaires, that they wished to do more than at present. Further research is needed in this area. However, it does appear that at least some schools and colleges value and wish to encourage pupil involvement, even though only a small number have involved their pupils in all the major areas of schooling, i.e. assessment, curriculum and decision making.

The findings indicate that the importance of pupil involvement is being recognized by schools, and increasingly policies for involvement are being developed. Where schemes have been implemented, the feedback provided by pupils has proved valuable. When pupils are consulted they have responded in a sensible and constructive manner. Nonetheless, work is needed in this area to discover new procedures and techniques for seeking the views and opinions of pupils and to improve existing ones (see also Gersch and Gersch, 1995).

## Some Innovative Projects

Over the past 12 years a number of projects aimed to increase the involvement of children in assessment and their school lives have been undertaken by the present authors. They are described more fully elsewhere, but are included to give an indication of some of the sorts of possible responses available to schools.

In one project, (Gersch and Noble, 1991) children were involved in a whole school systems change. The school was concerned about poor attendance and disenchantment in the Fifth Year (Year 11). A decision was reached to set up working groups with teachers and pupils, to examine the cause of the problems and to make suggestions. Interestingly, the consultation process itself improved communication within the school, motivated students and led to a substantial number of realistic and helpful practical recommendations.

In another classroom project, (Gersch and Brown, 1986; Gersch, 1990) children were simply given a form on which to record their work completed and their grade of how hard they had worked. The teacher then gave her own grading, which was linked to a reward system at the end of the week. The sheet was signed by the class teacher, head teacher and sent home. An evaluation study revealed that most children had enjoyed the system, worked harder and understood teacher grades more readily.

Other initiatives have included assisting with the development of a local council policy which placed listening to the learners as a central element.

## The Student Report

Since 1981 the author, together with a number of colleagues able to carry out evaluation projects as part of their training to become educational psychologists, (including Pauline Claridge and Amanda Holgate), have been developing formats which have aimed to offer children opportunities to express their views about their strengths, weaknesses, needs, plans and aspirations. Fuller accounts of these initiatives have been published elsewhere, e.g. Gersch and Cutting (1985). Gersch (1987; 1990; 1992), Gersch, Holgate and Sigston (1993).

There is little doubt that children really enjoy participating in this way, they say useful, constructive and relevant things, and the results have proved to be of value to those professionals providing advice about the children. Indeed, where decision making has been particularly difficult, or finely balanced, a student report has proved to be of immense value.

*A Child's Report for Children in Care*

The very first report produced was for children in care, entitled the Child Report (Gersch and Cutting, 1985). This was used as part of a multi-professional assessment, and proved to provide both helpful data to the decision making panel and also a useful vehicle for the child and careworker to discuss plans. We learnt then, however, that there was a definite need to provide guidelines and perhaps training for adults, and that children needed preparation for the task. The headings for this report were 'School, Home, Time at Peartree House (the residential home), Hobbies and Pastimes, and the Future'.

*Child's Report for Children Being Assessed under the 1981 Act*

The next format produced was the Child's Report devised for children who were being assessed under the 1981 Education Act and which could be used as the child's Advice. The target group was children who were between the age of 13 and 15, undergoing what was then called a 13+ re-assessment under the 1981 Act.

Given the support of the local education department and assistant education officer it was possible to include the report as part of the appendices to the Statement itself, and there were occasions when the officer wrote direct to the student, sending them a copy of their Statement for comments. The categories in this report were 'School Background, Present School, Special Needs, Friends, Hobbies, Interests and Out Of School Activities, The Future and Additional Comments'.

Overall, we found that children very much enjoyed giving their views, and again they produced sensible and constructive comments, which were of help to their teachers and other professionals. Careful evaluation of the materials, however, revealed that written guidance for adult helpers was essential, that the language needed to be modified, the form needed to be presented more attractively, and more space was needed for children to express their feelings. Also, the children told us that secondary pupils preferred to be called 'students'.

*The Student Report (1994)*

The report form was subsequently revised, both in 1991 and 1993 following use with children and an evaluation of their views about the form. We also had the good fortune to have the services of a graphic designer, Jack Rummins, with the result that we were able to publish the Student Report (1994) in a glossy booklet form, which we hope is attractive to those using it. Guidelines for adult helpers are included as the last page. The headings of this latest edition include 'School, Special Needs, Friends, Life Out Of School, Feelings, the Future, and Anything Else', and we are currently examining the development of an abbreviated version which could be used more readily as part of the appendices to the Statement.

## Other Techniques

Other workers have also been developing report formats for use with younger children. Mitchell (1993) has produced a format for the child to provide advice when undergoing formal assessment, entitled 'This is me' and Surrey Educational Psychology Service have also developed materials in the light of the Code of Practice. A useful pack to help children prepare for acting as witnesses in court is also available from the NSPCC (NSPCC, 1993).

## Processes of Development

It is perhaps worth re-iterating and stressing that the forms themselves have been adapted and changed in the light of consumer evaluation, piloting and experience.

The key steps that have proved useful are as follows:

1 define the aim of the assessment,
2 examine what techniques are being currently used,
3 consider ways of increasing active pupil participation,
4 draft some sort of format or response sheet for children,
5 provide guidance for adult helpers,
6 evaluate the format or report form over time and,
7 modify and update regularly.

## A Student Booklet for Excluded Pupils

The focus for this section is listening to the voice of the child who has been excluded from school and a small scale research project and practical outcomes, in the form of a booklet for students and a leaflet for parents, is described. For those wanting more information, the findings of this study have been reported more fully elsewhere (Gersch and Nolan, 1994).

The aim of this research was to gain an insight into pupils' views on exclusion and to use this insight to make recommendations to the borough about provision and procedures. A further aim of the project was to use the process and findings to develop practical tools which would act to increase pupil involvement. The sample consisted of six students (four male and two female), between the ages of 12 and 16, who had been permanently excluded from at least one school. The ethnic groups of the pupils, as described by their parents, were five UK and one African-Caribbean/UK. These students had all attended the borough's off-site provision and had experienced re-integration into another secondary school. The methodology used was qualitative research using individual semi-structured interviews. Many of the students had experienced difficulties with academic tasks and pupil relationships starting from primary school and had experienced frequent changes of primary school. All the students had suffered serious disruptions in their home lives, such as going into care or parental separations.

It was found that the students were angry about what had happened to them. They were not expecting to be excluded and did not know what was going to happen next. The months following an exclusion were often a very confusing and uncertain time for both the students and their families. However, they had found attending a small group provision to be helpful prior to reintegration; most developed positive relations with the unit teachers and felt that they gained an understanding of their feelings. The students did not understand the decision making processes involved in their admission to the unit and wanted a fresh start in a new school and looked to the support of both the new school staff and the outreach teachers in making a gradual start.

It is possible to summarize many of the findings in terms of a list of needs that the students identified for themselves: learning support; emotional support (e.g. counselling); behavioural support (e.g. clear guidelines); involvement in decision making at all stages; clear communication with parents and pupils; an advocate following exclusion; a small group environment to settle; a positive teacher relationship and support in gradual reintegration.

A variety of recommendations were made to the borough stemming from this research (e.g. the use of advocates for pupils and families, the clarification of procedures and decision making processes) and a working party on exclusions is incorporating the pupils' views in their work on new procedures and provision for students who have been excluded. A practical tool has also been developed in the borough, in the form of a student booklet named 'Where do I go from here? A booklet for students who have been excluded from school' (Nolan and Sigston, 1993). This booklet aims to encourage professionals and parents to seek the views of the students, to help the students reflect on what has happened and plan for their future. The student booklet is structured chronologically starting with the student's experiences in school, with work, teachers and other students. It goes on to ask about events leading up to the exclusion and linking consequences with behaviours. The students are asked about the actual exclusion and encouraged to reflect upon their own point of view and that of the school. They are then asked to consider reasons for their behaviour and any alternative ways of dealing with similar situations. Finally, the students are asked to identify what they may need in another school. The headings for 'Where do I go from here?' include 'My work, the teachers, the other kids, leading up to the exclusion, the exclusion itself, why I did what I did, and what am I looking for in another school'.

The booklet might be used by a pupil individually or with his or her family or carer. Educational psychologists, educational welfare officers or social workers could use it also as a guide for a structured interview. Teachers might use it after a fixed term exclusion or for a pupil reintegrating into their school. The pupil should be able to decide who works with them in completing the booklet and its distribution. A parents' leaflet has also been produced to inform parents of their rights and options when their child has been excluded.

### The Waltham Forest 'Assessment, Achievement and Action Project' (AAA)

This project is of particular interest since it resulted in an assessment procedure for schools, and indeed the borough as a whole, which places pupil involvement at the heart of the process. The project was set up in response to requests from schools and the LEA to provide a consistent set of procedures for schools to use when identifying, assessing and planning for children with special needs. The aim was to outline a borough procedure for schools. The outcome was a Handbook for Special Educational Needs Co-ordinators, which includes formats upon which children could record their work and views, and an agreed procedure for schools.

The project was undertaken in the London Borough of Waltham Forest during school years 1992/1993 and 1993/1994 and was led by members of the local Educational Psychology Service. The objectives of the project were to produce:

1   guidelines for schools on the early stages of assessment and intervention with children with special educational needs in mainstream schools
2   supporting documentation regarding record keeping about action taken, aims for the child and review dates
3   advice to the LEA about appropriate publicity and in-service training needed to implement the proposals.

#### Background

The project was undertaken in the context of the 1993 Education Act in which responsibilities and resources were being increasingly devolved to schools. During this time, the Department for Education were carrying out a consultation on the proposed Code of Practice for Special Educational Needs. As the AAA project progressed, it became increasingly clear from the drafts circulated for consultation by the DFE, that the Code was going to pay particular attention to the responsibilities of schools towards the estimated 18 per cent of children in mainstream schools who would have a special educational need at some time in their career, but not have the protection afforded by a Statement of Special Educational Needs.

*Forming the Work Group*

Against this background, it was crucial that LEA-wide procedures and policies should reflect not only good practice by schools but be 'owned' by the teachers and schools as well. To achieve this, groups of informed and interested staff from mainstream schools were formed by a process designed to mobilize support and commitment to the project, whilst keeping senior officers and elected members fully informed. If people were to listen to children, they must also have had the experience of being listened to and involved themselves.

The first step was to inform and obtain the backing of the then Acting Chief Education Officer for the project. In fact the idea had the full support of a special needs working party headed by the Acting CEO, who readily wrote to all schools inviting nominations for the work groups to undertake the project. When nominations were received, nominees were called to a training meeting which gave a thorough grounding in the origins of the project including the original recommendations of the Warnock Committee. Those who remained interested were asked to discuss the proposals in groups at the training meeting and then complete an information sheet as to the type of input they felt they could allocate to the project, realistically, given their existing commitments.

The project was undertaken by three groups in all — these were:

(a) The Task Group which drafted the materials. This group consisted mainly of experienced current practitioners (e.g. Special Needs Co-ordinators).

(b) The Consultation Group, also comprised of experienced current practitioners, which offered feedback and piloting for the materials produced.

(c) The Steering Group, which was chaired by the Principal Psychologist, and consisted of senior managers (e.g. head teachers from mainstream and special schools, heads of the borough special needs and multicultural support services, and the education officer with responsibility for special services). The Steering Group tackled the question of follow up training and support.

*Drafting the Handbook for Schools and Backup Material*

At the heart of the AAA process the groups produced a series of pupil questionnaires entitled 'Me and my work', to be completed by children themselves. Different versions of 'Me and my work' were produced for children of different ages and can be administered in a flexible manner. All versions of 'Me and my work' ask, right at the start of the assessment process, for the child or student's views on the work and situations they face at school and also explore with the child the type of help and support needed. The child is further consulted when an Individual Education Plan (IEP) is drawn up. The child also selects work for, and is involved in, subsequent progress reviews.

*The Outcome*

The end result was a booklet, produced by representatives of some quarter of the borough schools, entitled 'Assessment, Achievement Action: A Handbook for Special Educational Needs Co-ordinators; Procedures for planning and reviewing the progress of children and students with special educational needs in the London Borough of Waltham Forest (September 1994)'. This handbook has now been circulated to all the borough schools, and is available for use, albeit with modification, as an aid to schools in implementing the Code of Practice.

The booklet provides guidance about how to administer the Code of Practice Stages of Assessment, with supporting information on definitions, policies and bilingual children. There are sections which include diary sheets, action summaries, and examples of the pupil's work. Other forms elicit the child's feelings, views and attitudes and are as much to be completed, retained and owned by the pupil as the adults involved.

*Getting Support for AAA*

The first edition of the AAA materials was circulated to schools for piloting and comment. The draft handbook was also explained and presented at the borough's annual Special Needs Course and at specially convened meetings. Much of the feedback received was favourable although the length of the handbook (some 60 pages) has led to requests for a shorter form to be considered as a future project.

Using the management experience and guidance of the Steering Group, the AAA documents have now been commended by the Borough Education Committee as a basis for meeting the Code of Practice requirements in the borough's schools. AAA documents and formats are also cross-referenced in other parts of the LEA's response to the DFE Code of Practice, including forthcoming plans to conduct an annual audit of schools' arrangements for students with special educational needs as the basis for allocation of finance to schools.

Thus the child's point of view on learning difficulties is becoming incorporated into all the major systems of the borough including those key ones which determine finance, so often regarded as the bottom line. The principle of full pupil involvement has also been afforded the support of those at the highest decision making level; namely council and senior education officers. What is of particular note, when analyzing the process, is the number of schools who showed an interest, the benefits of schools working together on a project of mutual interest, the key involvement of practitioners who would have to use any guidance offered, and their involvement right from the start. The support of senior managers in the education department and indeed council itself was also seen as a critical feature in ensuring the success of the project.

## Some Complex Issues and Dilemmas

Listening constructively to children is more easily said than done; in reality there are many practical as well as moral problems which can arise. In this section, I wish to discuss a number of the issues which have frequently presented themselves. There are six main issues worth highlighting, as follows:

(a)  adults' attitudes,
(b)  the capability and maturity levels of children,
(c)  parent-child disputes,
(d)  'Who pays the piper. . . .',
(e)  changing one's mind; negotiating, counselling and exploring, and
(f)  what the child needs as opposed to says s/he wants.

### *Adults' Attitudes*

Some adults may hold a relatively deep-rooted view that 'children should be seen and not heard'. More frequently there can be a tendency to speak for children, override their opinions, or simply instruct them about what is needed. The fact is that in much of a child's life, instruction is the norm, and thus really listening to children is an exception. Adults may feel, with *some* justification that they know best about what the children need. The point worth making, however, is that there is a distinction between listening and simply doing what children say. There is scope to discuss ideas, and indeed for positions to be altered and compromises to be reached.

Some teachers do ask the children for their views, but feel that they (the teachers) should report these rather than giving the child a separate report. Doubtless some adults might fear that children will be embarrassing or unkind in their replies, or that they might not be capable of responding. Experience of work in this area has tended to allay such concerns.

In all this, much depends upon the atmosphere of the interview and discussions. We have all had experiences of certain people inviting us to speak freely but nonetheless leaving us feeling quite hesitant. Adults need to consider what they could do to create a truly listening ethos, communicating trust, respect, patience, openness, sincerity, warmth, and ways of adopting a non-judgmental style, inviting elaboration of ideas and exploring them, rather than using closed questions or worse, arguing back.

### *The Capability and Maturity Levels of Children*

Another key point often made by those who are critical of increased child involvement is that some children might not be capable of responding validly: they are too young, inexperienced. Indeed for those with severe special educational needs, there may be intellectual or other constraints to the child participating.

In the author's experience even very young children have been able to express their ideas and thoughts often with startling insight, and children and young people with severe learning difficulties are able to express preferences. The issue is how to tap these ideas and encourage children to express themselves. We do need to teach children how to articulate their views clearly and assertively, and adults how to listen. Psychoanalysts refer to the need to listen with an inner ear, and to separate the 'manifest' from 'latent' content, i.e. that which the child actually says versus what the child really means. We do need to use counselling skills to get to the latter. Nonetheless, whilst techniques, procedures and methods may need to be modified for different children, and the language will need to be suitable and accessible, there is scope for increasing the active involvement of all children in their learning, education, schooling. Further, the earlier we start the process the better.

Another point worth making is about children lying. It is of course inevitable that under certain circumstances people (adults and children) do exaggerate, they may withhold information or tell untruths. Although there may be individual differences in the tendency to do this, the question arises as to why it should occur and under what circumstances. Such behaviour may be a consequence of fear, anxiety or a wish to create impressions due to low confidence or self esteem. For some reason, people do seem to have attributed children with greater honesty, recall and powers of memory than adults, which is clearly not the case, but a balance does need to be struck. Overall it would seem that in a non-judgmental interview where children feel at ease and involved and safe, lying becomes unnecessary and less likely to occur.

### Parent-child Disputes

An interesting dilemma can arise if the views of the child differ from those of the parents, and further if decisions need to be made about the child's educational plans or programme. Obviously, much will depend upon the actual issue, but the Children Act is clear that professionals and courts should regard the welfare of the child as paramount. Obviously, the best recourse would appear to be making explicit the differences and attempting some form of reconciliation and compromise.

### Who Pays the Piper

For professionals who wish to be advocates for children, there can be real conflicts of interest. Consideration of the role of the employer, who is paying for the service, and the limitations of professional advocacy must be taken into account. Perhaps the time will come when, like financial advisers, professionals in the children's field will need to make explicit who is paying them and what the limits of their freedoms to advise might be!

Booth and Potts (1992) argue that professionals vary immensely in the way they work, and there are many obstacles to them partnering parents. The same obstacles could get in the way of their acting as child advocates. Their list includes conflicts of interests; unequal power relationships; obstacles to communication; misconceptions; lack of confidentiality and trust; and lack of time to build strong relationships. These authors also stress how far office resources make a difference; professionals have offices, phones, faxes, jargon, shorthand, access and lines of communication. Children have none of these. It is only right therefore for professionals to be clear about their limitations and the constraints to their role. Perhaps the best position is for the child to express himself or herself and for the professional to open up lines of communication for the child to do so.

### Changing One's Mind: Negotiating, Counselling and Exploring

Sometimes, children may not have experience about the issue upon which they are asked to comment. Ways need to be found to encourage children to explore new ideas and keep an open mind, before reaching conclusions. Children do need to learn negotiation techniques, ways of choosing and hypothesis testing and risk taking, as well as about probability and decision making.

### What the Child Needs as Opposed to Says S/he Wants

There is evidence that children's responses during interviews can be affected by the process itself (e.g. Armstrong *et al.*, 1993) and that the conditions have to be right to elicit valid responses. Cooper (1993) draws attention to such factors as the child's view of the aim of the interview, the way the assessment is managed, and the use to which the information is to be used, in influencing how far children will feel able to respond openly.

In the final analysis, decisions will need to be made about children, and there is nothing in the policy of maximizing children's active participation that denigrates the position of adults as responsible carers, and professionals arriving at their best professional judgment. In the final event, adults have the responsibility for making decisions in the child's best interests. However, the quality of such decisions is likely to be enhanced through the maximal involvement of the child.

## A Checklist for Schools and Teachers

Within most schools there is much that is already happening to involve pupils. The following checklist is offered as an *aide memoir* to assist further developments and planning:

*A. Identify and Audit What is Happening at Present to Include Pupils' Views in School Life*

1 Consider

(a) assessment processes

(b) the curriculum

(c) policy development

(d) general school life

(e) evaluation procedures

2 How are pupils views elicited at present?

(a) Are student report forms used?

(b) Do staff use interviews?; How is this reported?

(c) Is lesson time set aside for discussion with pupils about school developments?

(d) Do the pupils evaluate lesson materials, content, teaching arrangements, provision, etc.?

(e) Are views sampled with small groups of pupils?

(f) Is there a Pupil or School Council?

(g) Where should a child with a new idea take this idea?

(h) Are such ideas encouraged or discouraged?

3 Do you think the current methods of eliciting pupils' views in schools are sufficient?

4 What do the children think about how far their views are taken into account in school, either at a whole school level or in relation to their own assessments and planning, and individual education plans?

(a) Is a survey of their views needed?

(b) Could this be done by questionnaire?

(c) Could form lessons be used to discuss the issue?

(d) Should the issue be placed on a staff meeting agenda?

B. *Getting New Ideas*

(a) Trawl ideas from colleagues and other schools

(b) Brainstorm as a staff group

(c) Brainstorm with children

(d) Invite views of governing bodies

(e) Invite views of others e.g. parents, educational psychologists, specialist visiting teachers etc.

C. *Planning for Change*

(a) Discuss and agree a small number of manageable ideas for action, which can be achieved

(b) Identify who is going to do what, when and by what date, with what resources

(c) Is INSET needed for staff and also training and preparation for children?

(d) Produce a written plan

(e) Share with all concerned

(f) Ensure that the pupil involvement plan is integrated with other key school plans, e.g. the school development plan, special educational needs policy.

D. *For Children with Special Educational Needs*

Finally, for children with special educational needs reference should be made to the Code of Practice (p.15) as a last check to ensure that due regard has been given to all such guidance. Of particular note is the suggestion that schools should consider how they:

(a)   record pupil's views in identifying their difficulties, setting goals, agreeing strategies, monitoring and reviewing progress, and

(b)   involve pupils in implementing individual educational plans.

## A Checklist for LEAs

LEA officers will undoubtedly look to the schools to provide the major impetus to pupil involvement, but nonetheless there may be some things which can be undertaken at an LEA level which serve to increase the active involvement of children in assessment, particularly following the publication of the Code of Practice. The following list of questions appears to arise:

1   What is the LEA doing generally to include pupils views?

(a)   What are the main areas of LEA contact when children's views could be more actively included? e.g. school placements, exclusions, assessments of special educational needs, pupils' views about provisions and facilities, pupils' ideas about services provided by the LEA

2   Who are the key officers in these areas?

(a)   How far is there an integrated policy and philosophy on listening to children?

(b)   Is there a council policy on the subject?

3   Carry out an audit of the level of pupil participation at present, and ask whether more could be done. If so,

(a)   How could such actions be co-ordinated?

(b)   Who could take a lead role?

(c)   When could such actions be planned?

(d)   What is the attitude of the department as a whole?

(e)   What are the objections and obstacles to progress?

4   When assessing special educational needs, how far do the current practices include the views of the child?

(a)  Is a separate Student Report or Student Advice invited?

(b)  Is the Statement discussed with the child?

(c)  Is the Statement sent to the child?

(d)  Do children attend annual reviews?

(e)  Do they attend Panel meetings, where Panel meetings are held to discuss individual children?

(f)  Do LEAs in their guidance to schools encourage the involvement of children throughout the process?

(g)  When problems arise, are children's views invited?

(h)  Is feedback from pupils about the process invited?

(i)  Is consumer feedback from pupils utilized as a measure of performance?

## A Check List for Individual Non-teaching Professionals e.g. Educational Psychologists, Medical Advisers, Social Workers, Speech Therapists etc.

*A. General Attitude Towards Pupil Involvement*

(a)  In your work, how far do you feel it is important to listen to the views of children?

(b)  Do you have any concerns about involving children and are there any limitations to your listening to children?

*B. Methods and Techniques Used When Listening to Children*

(a)  What special methods or techniques are you currently using to elicit the views of children?

(b)  Do you explain your role and the purpose of your interview?

(c)  Do you give the child an opportunity to question the process, correct any misunderstandings, through asking questions about the assessment or your interview? Do you encourage such questioning?

(d)   Do you invite the child's views about the assessment?

(e)   Do you listen to their views about their treatment, provision or arrangements?

(f)   Do you record the child's views specifically?

(g)   Do you see children without parents being present?

(h)   How do you deal with a possible difference between the child's and parental view?

(i)   Do children ever tell you things in confidence,? How do you deal with this?

(j)   Do you discuss directly with children your findings, results, recommendations, treatment plans, and the reasons for referrals?

(k)   At reviews, do you invite children to comment about their progress?

### C. Personal Considerations

(a)   Do you have any training needs in the area of listening to children or pupil involvement?

(b)   How far are you able to act as an advocate for the child in representing his or her view to decision makers?

(c)   In what ways might you be able to increase the active involvement of children in their assessments or in their school life?

(d)   Do you think that the children you see are clear about your role, rationale for interview, place in the system and what happens next? Did you check this out with the children?

## Conclusions: Trends and Possible Future Developments

The Code of Practice has stressed the importance of involving pupils with special needs throughout the process of their assessments. It can be argued that there has been a major shift in attitudes in schools, families and society at large, whereby greater weight is now placed upon the importance of listening to children. However, one should not underestimate possible resistance to such ideas and changes. The challenge for the future is to develop techniques, methods and, most importantly, appropriate attitudes to undertake the task effectively.

True listening requires complex skills; the atmosphere has to be right, the relationship has to be right, trust has to be communicated. Adults may have to examine the literature on counselling, attend 'INSET' and deal with antipathetic attitudes from colleagues. For their part children may have to learn how to state their views in a polite, assertive yet sometimes challenging way.

The future would appear to be set for an increase in pupil involvement in all walks of life, and at school in particular. However, schools, teachers and professionals, are at different stages of their own development, and every school, teacher and professional will need to devise their own individual action plan to ensure that such developments as appear to be taking place are successful. Most importantly, although each plan will need to be individually tailored to the specific school or institutional setting, there is much that can be shared and developed without having to start right from the beginning

## Acknowledgments

I am indebted to all the school staff, children, trainee educational psychologists and educational psychologist colleagues who have taken part in the projects described in this chapter, and to the LEA officers and others for their assistance and wholehearted support. I am particularly grateful to Shirley Moyse, Anna Nolan and Graham Pratt for their help in drafting sections on (a) school attitudes to pupil involvement (b) excluded students and (c) the AAA project respectively. The views expressed in this chapter, however, and any errors in content, of course, remain those of the author alone. Such views do not necessarily represent those of the authority in which the author is employed or schools in which the work took place.

## References and Further Reading

ARMSTRONG, D., GALLOWAY, D. and TOMLINSON, S. (1993) 'Assessing special educational needs: The child's contribution', *British Educational Research Journal*, **19**, 2, pp.121–31.

BOOTH, T. and POTTS, P. ( 1992) *Learning For All*, (Course E242 Units 3/4. Learning from experience), Milton Keynes, Open University.

CLIFFORD, B.R. (1993) 'Witnessing: A comparison of adults and children', *Issues in Criminological and Legal Psychology*. No 20, pp.15–21.

COOPER, P. (1993) 'Learning from pupils' perspectives', *British Journal of Special Education*, **20**, 4, pp.129–33.

DAVIE, R. (1993) 'Listening to the child: A time for change', *The Psychologist*, **6**, 6, pp.252–57.

DFE (1994) *Code of Practice on the Identification and Assessment of Special Educational Needs*, London, Department for Education.

GERSCH, I.S. and CUTTING, M.C. (1985) 'The child's report', *Educational Psychology in Practice*, **1**, 2, pp.63–9.

GERSCH, I.S. and BROWN, K. (1986) 'Pupils self-graded work record sheet', in SHEARER, M., GERSCH, I.S. and FRY, L. (Eds) (1990) *Meeting Disruptive Behaviour*, London, Macmillan Educational.

GERSCH, I.S. (1987) 'Involving Pupils in their own assessment', in BOWERS, T. (Ed) *Special Educational Needs and Human Resource Management*, London, Croom Helm.

GERSCH, I.S. (1990) 'The Pupil's view', in SCHERER, M., GERSCH, I.S. and FRY, L. (Eds) *Meeting Disruptive Behaviour: Assessment, Intervention and Partnership*, London, Macmillan Educational.

GERSCH, I.S. and NOBLE, J. (1991) 'A Systems project involving students and staff in a secondary school', *Educational Psychology in Practice*, **7**, 3, pp.140–47.

GERSCH, I.S. (1992) 'Pupil involvement in assessment', in CLINE, T. (Ed) *The Assessment of Special Educational Needs: International Perspectives*, London, Routledge.

GERSCH, I.S., HOLGATE, A. and SIGSTON, A. (1993) 'Valuing the child's perspective: A revised student report and other practical initiatives', *Educational Psychology in Practice*, **9**, 1, pp.36–45.

GERSCH, I.S. and NOLAN, A. (1994) 'Exclusions — what the pupils think', *Educational Psychology in Practice*, **10**, 1, pp.35–45.

GERSCH, I.S. and HOLGATE, A. (1991; 1994) *The Student Report*, London Borough of Waltham Forest.

GERSCH, I.S. and GERSCH, B. (1995) 'Supportive advocacy and self advocacy: The role of the allied professions', in GAINER, P. and SANDOW, S. (Eds) *Advocacy, Self Advocacy and Special Needs*, London, David Fulton.

MILES, M.B. and HUBERMAN, A.M. (1984) *Qualitative Data Analysis*, Sage Publications.

MITCHELL, S. (1993) 'This is me: A format for the child to provide personal advice when undergoing formal assessment', Placement project report as part of MSc professional training in educational psychology, University of East London.

NOLAN, A. and SIGSTON, A. (1993) *Where Do I Go From Here?* A booklet for students who have been excluded from school, The London Borough of Waltham Forest.

NSPCC (1993) *The Child Witness Pack*, London, NSPCC/Childline.

SURREY COUNTY COUNCIL (1994) *Involving the Child*, Teachers' Pack, My Learning Report 1, 2 and 3.

UNITED NATIONS (1989) *Convention on the Rights of the Child*.

WHITE, R., CARR, P. and LOWE, N. (1990) *A Guide to the Children Act 1989*, London, Butterworths.

# 3    A Social Work Perspective*

*Peter M. Smith*

### Introduction

Over the past ten years the weight given in law to the wishes and feelings of the child has increased. Many social work decisions are made within the legal framework of the Children Act 1989 which in specific areas extends children's rights to make decisions about their own futures. The Act also places a stronger emphasis on consulting with children about decisions even where it is adults in the end who will make the decision. The law is too blunt a tool to determine which decisions children can make for themselves. It is often a matter for the professional judgment of social workers, when to make decisions in agreement with a child's own view, and when to hear the child's view but proceed to make a different decision on behalf of the child.

This chapter examines the balance struck in the Children Act between a child's right to be consulted and a child's right to decide; presents some recent evidence about social work practice in ascertaining children's wishes and feelings; and concludes by offering some practice indicators for finding out children's views.

### The Children Act 1989

A good place to start is to ask what the law requires of social workers and what are the reasons for these requirements. The Children Act 1989 creates a common framework for all court decisions about the care and upbringing of children except for adoption which is currently the subject of government review. The Children Act (Section 1(3)) lays down a checklist of factors which the court must consider when it is making a decision about a child; at the top of the list is 'the ascertainable wishes and feelings of the child (considered in the light of his age and understanding)'. While the court must find out, and then must consider the child's wishes and feelings, such wishes and feelings are not decisive. The 'paramount consideration' for the court shall be 'the child's welfare' (Section 1(1)). This is essentially a paternalistic decision by the adults concerned,

---

* n.b. The views expressed in this chapter are those of the writer and not of the Department of Health.

the judge, or the magistrates with advice from social workers and others. The Children Act may have been called a charter for children and been held responsible for handing too much power to children, but a careful reading of what the Children Act actually says demonstrates that children have an increased voice in proceedings, not the decisive word.

Social workers also have to make decisions outside the court arena, in particular about children who are looked after by local authorities. When social workers make decisions about a child who is looked after, or indeed is about to be looked after, the law is quite specific about which considerations must bear on decisions (Section 22). Again at the top of the list are the ascertainable wishes and feelings of the child concerned having regard to the child's age and understanding. Not only must the child be consulted but also the child's parents and other people whom the local authority think are relevant. This can include children. Older and younger siblings and friends can have a very deep understanding and intimate knowledge of the circumstances of the child in question. The law allows for such consultation with children.

Before any decisions can be taken the social worker must give due consideration 'to the child's religious persuasion, racial origin, and cultural and linguistic background'. It is not acceptable for social services departments to ignore the individual background characteristics of children whom they are looking after. Sensitivity to issues of race and culture should therefore run through decision making for children.

For each child looked after by a local authority there has to be a regular series of reviews to ensure that the child's progress is properly monitored and future plans are made. The Department of Health Regulations and Guidance (DH, 1991) spells out practice requirements to give the child a voice. The Review Regulations require that:

- Before any review the authority shall as far as is practicable seek and take into account the views of the child and parents and other people (Regulation 7(1)).
- The authority shall so far as is practicable involve the persons whose views are sought in the review . . . (Regulation 7(2)).

The prominence of the child's voice in the sections cited above should be considered in the context of other requirements dispersed throughout the Act. As is pointed out more fully elsewhere (Smith, 1991), 'Apparently unconnected and disparate parts of the Act flow together to strengthen the participation of children in decisions made about them'.

The emphasis on consulting with children in the Children Act is consistent with the relevant articles of the UN Convention on the Rights of the Child. Article 12 requires that all countries agreeing to the Convention 'shall assure to the child who is capable of forming his or her own views the right to express those views freely in all matters affecting the child, the views of the child being given due weight in accordance with the age and maturity of the child'.

In a limited number of areas the Children Act increases the power of older adolescents to act autonomously. For example young people aged 16 and 17 who are looked after by local authorities as a result of voluntary agreements between their parents and the Social Services can refuse their parents' demand that they should return home. This has helped a number of young people who have been happily settled in foster homes to resist pressure from parents to go home. A second example is the power of young people to refuse certain types of 'medical or psychiatric examination or assessment' if they 'have sufficient understanding to make an informed decision' (Section 38(6)). In such limited circumstances the voice of the child is decisive, provided of course that the child can convince the authorities that they have 'sufficient understanding to make an informed decision'.

Thirdly, the Act gives children the right to ask the court's permission to make their own applications for courts to make a decision about something which is troubling them. For example a child could apply for a Specific Issue Order to determine some aspect of the child's upbringing, for example, which school a child should attend or whether a child should undergo a medical operation. The court will only give its permission for the application to be heard if it thinks that the child has sufficient understanding to make the application. This is a significant advance for children who previously would not have been able to initiate court proceedings. However the intention of Parliament was clearly not to provide ready access to law for children who may be in dispute with their parents over possibly trivial matters. A child's path to legal redress is littered with opportunities for paternalistic judgment. How will a court decide that a child has 'sufficient understanding' to make an application? Usually a solicitor will make this case to the court and a solicitor is not always someone well versed in child development. Often social workers are not involved in such cases, and before children can persuade a solicitor to try to persuade a court that they have sufficient understanding they will generally have to convince the Legal Aid Board that their case has merit, unless they are independently wealthy. Despite these obstacles it is important that social workers, teachers, youth workers and others are aware of the legal provisions intended to enable children to bring problems to a court for resolution.

In one example a thirteen year old girl, referred to as CT, started her own case which went all the way to the Court of Appeal. CT had been adopted but was having problems with her adoptive family and so she was being looked after by Social Services. She was in contact with her birth family and wanted the court to consider if she might return to them. Her adoptive parents tried to stop her making her own application but the Court of Appeal allowed CT's case to go forward. In this case the Court of Appeal did not act paternalistically but supported a 13 year old's right to make her own application.

A review of the debates while the Children Bill passed through the Houses of Parliament provides some insights into the reasons for the present legal balance between children's rights to decide and a paternalistic determination of children's welfare. A fundamental principle was established by the Gillick judgment in 1986 where the House of Lords decided that a child under the age of 16 could receive medical treatment without the consent of her parents provided that she had the maturity to understand the implications of her decision (Gillick v. West Norfolk and Wisbech Area Health Authority [1985] 3 AER 402). A key part of the judgment reads:

[An underlying principle of the law] is that parental right yields to the child's right to make his own decisions when he reaches a sufficient understanding and intelligence to be capable of making up his own mind on the matter requiring decision.

Lord Scarman in his judgment went on to say:

The law relating to parent and child is concerned with problems of growth and maturity and the human personality. If the law should impose on the process of growing up fixed limits, where nature knows only a continuous process, the price would be artificiality and lack of realism in an area where the law must be sensitive to human development and social change.

This judgment was an important reference point for the Parliamentary debates on the Children Bill. The Children's Legal Centre prepared amendments to the Bill to bring the Gillick principle into statutory law. One amendment proposed that the child's view should determine the matter in dispute provided that the child had sufficient understanding to make an informed judgment and the court was satisfied that allowing the child's voice to be decisive would not prejudice the child's welfare. This amendment was defeated because of the fear that the wishes and feelings expressed by a child would be overly influenced by the views of the parent or carer with whom the child lived. Increasing the weight in law to be given to the wishes of the child runs the risk of increasing the burden on the child who would be under greater duress to express to the court the views of one parent. The Lord Chancellor explained the Government's position:

It is very difficult to get this exactly right but, bearing in mind the very real risks of embroiling children in disputes which have been stirred up between their parents, the Bill. . . . strikes the right balance between giving proper weight to the child's view while avoiding burdening him with invidious decisions and putting so much of a premium on his decision that a parent might be tempted to take steps to try to secure that decision.
In principle it is surely right to take the child's interest as the paramount consideration and to subsume in that a consideration of the child's wishes.' (Hansard, House of Lords, Col 1154, 19 December 1988)

Thus the law retains a strong paternalistic thread in order to protect children. It also respects children as human beings in their own right with their own individual views and feelings. It is clear that the child's wishes are not to be dismissed or belittled simply because they are those of a child. A child's voice should be heard and carefully conveyed to decision makers who should listen.

In public law cases, that is where there is a dispute between the state and a family about the care and upbringing of a child, for example, in care proceedings, guardians ad litem are invariably appointed for the child. One of the main duties of the guardian ad litem is to ascertain the wishes and feelings of the child and to present them to the court. In private law cases, that is, where there are disputes between private individuals about the care and upbringing of a child, for example contact or residence, often a court welfare officer will be appointed. The welfare officer is bound by the checklist in the Children Act which is headed by the child's wishes and feelings. There are similarities and differences between the roles of guardians ad litem and court welfare officers. Both are officers of the court, are bound by the checklist in their reporting and tend to be social workers by training. At the moment court welfare officers are part of the Probation Department and guardians ad litem are mostly self-employed members of Panels of Guardians ad Litem, organized by local authorities. Key differences are that guardians are parties in care proceedings, and therefore have legal representation, and also are required by court rules to help the court with the management of the case, for example by advising about setting a realistic timetable to hear the case.

While court welfare officers and guardians are charged with particular responsibilities to ascertain the wishes and feelings of children, all child care social workers have similar responsibilities as outlined by the discussion of Section 22 of the Children Act above. The next section addresses what we know from Social Services Inspections and recent research about how social workers are going about their business of finding out the wishes and feelings of children.

### Evidence of Social Work Practice

The Social Services Inspectorate's first inspection of the guardian ad litem service since the implementation of the Children Act found that guardians followed Department of Health advice and separately recorded the wishes and feelings of children in their court reports. Guardians reported that they experienced most difficulty in working with the 6–10 year age group and that there was a danger that the views of children in this age group could be inappropriately discounted. Although a mostly positive picture emerged of consulting with children, SSI identified as a key issue the need for guardians ad litem to develop their skills in direct communication with children (SSI, 1994a).

It is in private proceedings that more concern has been expressed about making the child's views heard. One small study of court welfare practice before the Children Act examined the priority given to finding out children's views.

Court Welfare Officers were asked to rank order thirteen different aims when preparing a report. Telling the court what the child wanted was ranked twelfth leaving the author to conclude that 'many children remain unseen, unheard and waiting on the sidelines for a decision to be made about their future' (Kingsley, 1990). This is a worrying finding because of the weight given by the court to the recommendations of the welfare officer, which is illustrated by the requirement on magistrates to record their reasons fully if they do not agree with the welfare officer's recommendation.

In recent years most social work with children has come under the heading of child protection. Often social work practice has been criticized for failing to find out the wishes and feelings of children and also for failing to give proper weight to those views which have been ascertained. The Report by Lord Justice Butler-Sloss on Child Abuse in Cleveland was critical of social workers' interviews of children and made a number of recommendations, particularly about interviewing children who have alleged sexual abuse (Lord Justice Butler-Sloss, 1988).

More recent reports into social work in child protection continue to raise questions about social workers' tendencies not to interview children and to make assumptions about children's feelings 'which were not supported by the evidence' (SSI, 1994b). Farmer and Owen (1995) undertook a more in depth study of consumer views of the child protection process. Their interviews with older children paint a picture with a number of worrying features which question just how child-centred child protection interventions are. This picture also demonstrates the complexity of providing services which are sensitive to children's views and afford an appropriate level of protection from further abuse. The researchers reported:

> During investigations children felt that their disclosure or the discovery
> of abuse had unleashed a process over which they had no control. They
> had rarely been consulted or even informed about what to expect.

Children often blamed themselves for the process they had unwittingly unleashed, felt that they were responsible for whatever happened to the perpetrator and believed that their placement in care was a punishment. Children were grateful for counselling to explore their feelings in a non-blaming setting. Some sexually abused children regretted disclosing the abuse especially when it led to rejection by their families. Children struggled with simultaneous and conflicting emotions about abusive parents, loyalty and hatred, love and anger. Most young people wanted the abuse to stop. They did not want separation from their families. This research underlined children's awareness of any negative feelings about their parents held by social workers and how such negativity undermined the chances of forming working relationships with the children.

Another area of social work which is attracting a high level of public attention is residential care. There is greater recognition in some quarters of the importance of the consumer's view of the care provided. In its inspections of residential care SSI has included in its inspection teams young people who have lived in residential homes. These young people have been valuable in communicating with the young residents and in making judgments about the quality of care. A recent Report (DH, 1994c) found that children were encouraged to take part in planning meetings and reviews but children said they would have liked more say about the daily running of the home. Interestingly, where children were more involved in running the home, parents were more involved also. The Report recommends that 'regular meetings with children in all homes should be introduced to encourage children to contribute actively to the running of the home (p. 18)'.

Neither the inspection into residential care nor the inspection into services for disabled children (DH, 1994d) found that consultation with children paid adequate attention to their racial and cultural needs. With disabled children there was often little or no attempt to find out and record their views as if the presence of a disability somehow obviated the need for proper consultation.

Thus, while there is evidence of good practice in ascertaining the wishes and feeling of children in, for example, some residential homes and by many guardians ad litem, the overall picture is patchy and illustrates the need for social workers to pay greater attention to consulting with children.

### Indicators for Social Work Practice

The previous sections have indicated that social work practice is lagging behind legal expectations of consultation with children. This section offers a few practice indicators for social workers to consider when planning an interview to ascertain the wishes and feelings of a child.

Much of the recent literature about interviewing children has focused on investigative interviews. The main purpose of such interviews is to elicit information about events in a form which is likely to lead to the conviction of offenders in a criminal court. This is very different from the purpose of most social work interviews with children which will have, in part, the objective of finding out the wishes and feelings of the child. Nevertheless the guide to investigative interviewing, known as the Memorandum of Good Practice (Home Office, 1982), helpfully reminds the interviewer of the importance of paying attention to the child's

use of language,
emotional, social and cognitive development,
racial, cultural and religious background,
ability to trust adults and understand confidentiality,
level, if any, of disability or learning difficulties which may affect communication and
likely attention span and concept of time.

The Memorandum of Good Practice is directed at interviews which have to comply with strict rules regarding evidence. Most social work interviews should be more flexible, informal and guided by a casework rather than a legalistic framework. (See, for example, Garrett, 1982.)

### Purpose

It is essential that before the interview the social worker thinks about the purpose or purposes of the interview. The main purpose may be therapeutic, advisory, consultative or, infrequently, to gather evidence. Often a single interview will have a number of phases in which different purposes are to the fore. What follows is directed primarily at the consultative interview where a primary purpose is to find out the wishes and feelings of a child.

### Timing

What has the child done immediately before the interview, what will the child be doing afterwards and what is the child not doing as a result of having to be interviewed? If a social worker is interviewing an 11 year old child after school, at say 5.30, and finds him or her uncommunicative, is this because the child has difficulties in self-expression, or perhaps does not trust the interviewer, or would simply rather be watching a television soap opera or eating tea. While such questions may appear mundane or obvious, they will generally influence the child's presentation at interview and therefore the conclusions of the interviewer. This is equally true of events preceding or following the interview which may cause the child excitement or anxiety. If a child is interviewed following prolonged exposure to a foster family who freely express their disapproval of the foster child's parents, how much will the views expressed by the child be held genuinely? Court Welfare Officers are particularly aware of the changeability of the views of children who are caught in the crossfire of their parents' divorce.

### Ambivalence

Social workers must be able to reassure children that it is quite acceptable and normal that they want conflicting things at the same time (to live with ·Mum and to stay with foster carers) and to change their minds with some speed and frequency without being able to articulate the reasons. Ambivalence is often apparent through incongruence between the spoken word and the non-verbal message. For example, some children express their desire for contact in a monotone as if reciting flatly something committed to memory. Other children may express a wish for contact and yet sit quietly throughout the session withdrawn deeply into their own thoughts. Ambivalence also manifests itself by saying different things to different people at different times.

### Questioning and Questioner

After the initial phase to establish some rapport, the next phase of the interview should be asking open-ended questions. To ascertain the wishes and feelings of a child the aim is to trigger a child's stream of consciousness about the subject of interest to the interviewer. The open-ended question 'How are you getting on at home?' allows children to talk about anything on their minds about home, it could be Mum, Dad, siblings, neighbours, food, health, the cat or whatever. A more specific question 'How are you getting on with Dad?' directs the child's attention to his or her father which may or may not be welcome. Some resistance to the interview may be immediately triggered. The question which is open is more likely to enable expression of what is most in the mind of the child. If the interviewer defines the area of interest too early or too narrowly then the interviewer may never get on the same wave length as the child.

Clearly if a child does not spontaneously address a particular subject as a result of open-ended questions more specific questioning will have to follow. By observing the child's reactions carefully and following the child's pace, it is often possible to ease into the subject of most interest to the interviewer. This may be the subject which causes the most pain for the child, for example when consulting children about future living arrangements or contact with family.

Judges have frequently criticized social workers for asking a question and implicitly supplying the answer at the same time. For example, 'Are you not going to send your Mum a present?' or, 'Is it your Dad's shouting which makes you so frightened?' The phrasing of the first question implies the questioner's preferred response, that is, to send a present. The second question assumes information which the child may not have already shared, that is, the child is frightened and the fright is linked to Dad's shouting.

In seeking to understand children's views social workers often seek the child's reasons for a particular attitude or behaviour. The question 'Why?' must be dreaded by many children. Often children honestly do not know, or cannot articulate, why they feel or act in a certain way. Faced with incomprehension interviewers are tempted to offer an answer. For example, 'Did you beat up your little brother because you were angry that your Dad bought him a big present?' If the child agrees with this proffered answer it may indicate

1  the interviewer has helpfully put into words a child's genuine feeling, or
2  the child agrees in the absence of another explanation, or
3  the child wishes to bring the interview closer to an end, or
4  the child thinks it advisable to comply with the perceived preference of the interviewer.

The interpretation of the meaning of the child's agreement in such circumstances is rather subjective. Confident, or perhaps arrogant, workers may tend to conclude their professional insight allowed the child to deepen understanding of behaviour. The more self-aware or critical social worker may ask a number of contextual questions to help understand the meaning of the child's response. If the child is female and Bengali and the interviewer is male, white and wears a suit, does this suggest that the expressed agreement derives from a wish to please and comply with the apparent views of the interviewer? Paying full attention to racial and cultural factors is essential if the meaning of an interaction is not to be distorted by eurocentric assumptions.

The nature of the relationship between the child and interviewer is crucial to the understanding of the interaction. Social workers have to earn the trust of the children they interview. Issues of race and gender are important. A young woman may have good reason not to trust males in positions of power. Children of refugee families may have a deep mistrust of all officials from a foreign culture.

The matter of trust is closely tied to the question of confidentiality and a child's understanding of how far information given to a social worker will travel. Often social workers are eliciting the wishes and feelings of a child to enable the court to make a decision in the child's best interests. It is a principle of justice that all parties should be informed of the reason for decisions. In care proceedings the child's views form part of the evidence. Children must be informed and will often quickly grasp that their views will be made known to the parties including the parents. This creates a dilemma. A child may decide not to disclose his or her own views in order to protect parents from the pain of learning the child does not wish to live with or see the parent. Or children may misrepresent their views to protect their parents.

### Materials

Through training, social workers should have the opportunity of becoming more familiar and confident with different materials through which younger and less verbal children can express themselves. Conversation alone is rarely sufficient to find out the views of children under ten. Children express themselves through play with dolls, puppets and through drawing. With training and practice social workers become comfortable with different methods. Social workers and other professions working with children have been strongly reminded in court of the limitations of interpretations of children's expressive play. The value of drawings and other methods is as an extra source of information which may appear to confirm an existing understanding of a child's view or to suggest another avenue for further enquiry. Relying solely on interpretations of expressive material carries some risk of misconstruing a child's view. In association with other information such interpretations can be a valuable adjunct to consulting with children.

*Training*

The importance of training in communicating with children is recognized in the developments by the Care Sector Consortium and CCETSW to identify competencies expected of social workers in National Vocational Qualifications and the Diploma in Social Work. The components of good consultation with children are being identified in concrete form. This should enable practice supervisors and trainers to help workers identify strengths and weaknesses in particular aspects of the consultation process. Such developments in training are essential if the expectations established in law are to be achieved in practice.

## Conclusion

The Children Act reflects increasing public awareness of the importance of consulting with children. It is also a powerful lever to require that courts and social workers reach higher standards in ascertaining the wishes and feelings of children. The Act does not allow courts and social workers to find out the child's wishes and feelings and then to withdraw as if that were the end of the matter. This would be an abdication of adult responsibility. Once the child's wishes and feelings are known they are weighed with other factors, especially the child's maturity and level of understanding, in a decision where the child's welfare is paramount. There is evidence of good social work practice in consulting with children. However, there are also indications of where improvements are necessary, for example, in working with disabled children and with black and minority ethnic children.

## References

Butler-Sloss, Lord Justice (1988) *Report of the Inquiry into Child Abuse in Cleveland 1987*, London, HMSO.

Department of Health (1991) *The Children Act 1989 Guidance and Regulations*, Vol 3, London, HMSO.

Farmer, E. and Owen, O. (1995) *Decision-Making, Intervention and Outcome in Child Protection Work*, London, HMSO.

Garrett, A. (1982) *Interviewing, Its Principles and Methods*, New York, Family Services Association of America.

Gillick v West Norfolk and Wisbech Area Health Authority (1985) 3 AER 402.

Hansard (1988) House of Lords, Col 1154, December 19.

Home Office with Department of Health (1992) *Memorandum of Good Practice on Video Recorded Interviews with Child Witnesses in Criminal Proceedings*, London, HMSO.

Kingsley, J.R.K. (1990) 'The best interests of the child? The role of the court welfare officer', *Children and Society*, **4**, 3, pp.284–92.

Smith, P.M. (1991) 'The child's voice', *Children and Society*, **5**, 1, pp.58–66.

SOCIAL SERVICES INSPECTORATE (1994a) *Guardian ad Litem Services, A Report of the Findings and Key Issues Arising from an Inspection of 3 Panels*, London, Department of Health.

SOCIAL SERVICES INSPECTORATE (1994b) *National Overview Report of Child Protection Inspections*, London, Department of Health.

SOCIAL SERVICES INSPECTORATE (1994c) *Corporate Parents, Inspection of Residential Child Care Services in 11 Local Authorities*, London, Department of Health.

SOCIAL SERVICES INSPECTORATE (1994d) *National Inspection Report of Services for Disabled Children and Their Families*, London, Department of Health.

# 4   Eliciting Children's Views: the Contribution of Psychologists

*Neil Hall*

## Introduction

Identifying and comprehending the wishes and feelings of children could effectively be considered a basic process of the applied child psychologist's work. For those professional psychologists working with children and young people in statutory contexts, it can be assumed that they have always had a duty to assess the child's views of their circumstances. Moreover, as Davie (1993) has predicted, 'the signs point clearly to an increasing likelihood of psychologists being used much more frequently in child care and family law cases. The reason for this trend is that the law — even the criminal justice system — is becoming discernibly more child centred' (p.52).

The most useful psychological perspective which can be constructed here is one which amalgamates ideas from psychologists — researchers and clinicians — whose work, in collaboration with others from different disciplines, is directed at enhancing the skills of a range of professionals who actively seek the views of children — whether they are pupils, patients, witnesses or suspects. Specifically, this will relate to the following three topics:

(i)   children as witnesses (i.e. their reliability);
(ii)   interviewing children for legal reasons (i.e. maximizing the perspective of children);
(iii)   emotional trauma and children's memory (i.e. how remembering is affected by the experience of traumatic events).

Together, these factors form a theoretical, and a practice-based, psychological perspective the content of which could be variously implemented by a range of professionals who have a statutory responsibility for ascertaining the wishes and feelings of children.

Applied psychologists, and other professionals, involved in statutory work need generally to understand the nature of children's memory, behaviour and development, in a manner made obvious because of recent changes in legislation, research in applied psychology, current controversies about repressed memories, and increased numbers of reported allegations of child sexual abuse based on recovered memories. Aspects of children's memory are considered here as a central feature of the psychological perspective which, when modified to suit their own particular work settings, different professional groups can utilize when attempting to obtain and examine children's views.

## Children as Witnesses: Some Issues

The study of children as witnesses has long been a focus of researchers, whereas the techniques used for interviewing children have received less attention (Davies, 1994). However, Spencer and Flin (1990) have shown that comprehending the reliability of children's eyewitness testimony, and the methods used to interview children in legal contexts, are inextricably inter-linked, given that the quality and reliability of children's evidence is heavily dependent upon the skills of the interviewer. Moreover, effective and forensically relevant interviews with children (those which are acceptable for legal purposes) are only likely to arise when due consideration is given to the child's age, linguistic abilities and cognition (i.e. how they think and what they know), and other salient developmental factors for individual situations (Ornstein, 1991). Undoubtedly, the impetus for such research has been provided by the need of not only psychologists, but many other professionals, such as lawyers, the police, paediatricians, and social workers, who have required greater clarity and direction about investigating allegations of child sexual abuse (Jones, 1993). This work has necessarily been focused within a context of criminal proceedings, but there appears to be a case for this process to be made available for more general use in a range of educational, health, youth justice, and social care settings. Therefore, whilst the focus has been upon forensic issues (for the purposes of court proceedings in criminal cases) the psychological perspective can be applied to a broader spectrum of interview settings within statutory contexts.

The reliability of eye-witness testimony has always been an issue in the context of the criminal justice system, but it is principally from the perspective of the child witness that most recent psychological research and legal debate have flowed (Stephenson, 1992). Just as with elderly adults, this research has shown that young children have been wrongly assumed not to be able accurately to remember events as they occurred. Children's reports of what they have seen and or experienced, what it might have meant to them, how they might have been influenced to think differently from how they personally felt, and the details they have stored in memory and then recalled have, too frequently, been doubted, given reports of child witnesses failing to be acceptable to courts in criminal trials (as in the research reported by Ceci, Ross and Toglia, 1989; Dent and Flin, 1992).

The significance for the debate about gaining access, and giving credit, to the voice of the child centres on a range of often falsely held beliefs by adults, not only about the developmental aspects of children's cognition (their capacity for knowing and the limits of their thinking), especially their memory skills (Spencer and Flin, 1990), but also of their self-understanding (Stein and Jewett,

1986); the capabilities children have for providing reports about the meaning of their personal experiences (Heiman, 1992); the ways in which interviewers prevent children from stating their version of events (Evans and Webb, 1993); the impact of crime and other trauma on children, whether they have been victims and or witnesses (Johnson, 1989; Morgan and Zedner, 1992) and the nature of children's truth-telling and ability to tell lies (Morton, 1988).

Data on the reliability of children's evidence derives from a variety of research methodologies (Davies, 1995):

(i) staged events: where young children observe an unexpected incident, such as a stranger rushing into and out of a classroom, and are then questioned about what they saw — illustrating that a child's initial, freely-stated account of events is generally accurate, and that errors occur when leading questions are used to begin an interview (e.g. Ceci, 1994);

(ii) diary studies: when parents observe and record the behaviour of their own children they tend to provide data which support the view that young children usually provide less information about routine events, even when directly questioned, than they do about those which are new and unfamiliar.

(iii) naturally occurring stressful events: as in visiting the dentist or the doctor for treatment or inoculations (e.g. Goodman, Rudy, Bottoms and Aman, 1990); and

(iv) case histories: as with reports arising from the Cleveland (Butler-Sloss, 1988), Rochdale and Orkney (Clyde, 1992) inquiries, which generally illustrate how strongly held beliefs by professionals can seriously prejudice their ability to listen to and observe what children are actually saying and doing.

A common feature of these reports, and a point about which all professionals working with children need to be aware, concerns the potential for children being suggestible (see Ceci and Bruck (1993) for a review). As a psychological process, suggestibility encompasses a very wide range of ways in which individuals are thought of as being open to having their views shaped by others. Ceci (1994) describes how young children, when questioned about the same event during ten successive weekly sessions, provide reports about matters in which they apparently believe yet clearly exemplify that they are falsely remembering events which never took place. The process is as easily controlled by an adult's as by another child's suggestion, as it can equally apply to any situation in which there is a sufficient power imbalance to render a person disadvantaged — the image of a younger child being bullied by an older child into undertaking actions which they do not wish to perform is easy to construct, as is the similar cruelty displayed by some children to others who have learning disabilities and or other special needs.

In summary, research into children as witnesses informs professionals that children unintentionally tend to omit details in their account of events, rather than invent or deliberately tell lies about what has not happened; that children will also inadvertently produce incorrect information if they feel under pressure by either the nature of the adult's questions and or the power/authority of the adult; that children can identify and appropriately respond to deliberately mis-leading questions in contexts of naturally occurring stress but can frequently be coerced into keeping and maintaining secrets about high-stress inducing events as in situations where they are being abused; and that children will alter their original account of an event and produce so-called false memories if they are repeatedly questioned about the same matter.

### Interviewing Children for Legal Reasons: Some Current Trends

The significance for professionals seeking to obtain the views of children is that they must be aware of the many power differentials inherent in their contact with children: the negative consequences of repetitive questioning; the use of bribes and coercive tactics, no matter how benignly they are intended; and the potential for inducing stereotypical and expected responses. Steward *et al.* (1993) state that,

> The use of suggestive questioning can lead to errors in children's re-ports, but it is easier to mislead children about some types of informa-tion than about other types of information. For example, it may be relatively easy to mislead a 4-year old about details such as the color of someone's shoes or eyes, but more difficult to mislead the same child about personally significant events such as whether the child was hit or undressed. (p.27)

As Davies (1995) suggests, 'Questioners should cease blaming children for being suggestible and examine their own procedures for inappropriate and potentially misleading styles of questioning' (p.3).

The Memorandum of Good Practice (Home Office/Department of Health, 1992) establishes a code of professional practice, and sets minimum criteria for the video-recording of interviews of children in criminal proceedings where physical and or sexual abuse is at issue and where it is necessary to be consistent with the rules of evidence in courts of law. Many important messages about structuring and processing interviews are contained within the Memorandum and these are of much use in the wider context of interviewing children. As such, the document is an important resource for a variety of professionals who work with children and who aim to identify and explore children's viewpoints on significant matters affecting their lives. The imperative for interviewers working within the guidelines of the Memorandum, because of the rules of evidence, is that they must not be seen to pre-judge the issue and therefore to allow the facts obtained to speak for themselves.

The Memorandum, derived in part from research into developmental aspects of the psychology of children's memory (Davies, 1994), suggests structures and protocols for interviews wherein children can be helped to provide information about events which have been the source of their abusive experiences. Planning for the interview is a cornerstone of the Memorandum's advice: 'Failure to do so is likely to lead to an unsuccessful interview and consequent disservice to the interests of the child and justice' (Home Office/DOH, 1992, p.9). Clearly defined objectives for each interview are a minimum requirement. A thorough appreciation of a full range of developmental and cultural factors relating to each individual child is also demanded. Interviewers need an understanding of the child's cognition (e.g. their memory behaviour and attention span); language (e.g. how the child's language has developed; what regularly used words and phrases are peculiar to the individual child — of particular importance in relation to sexual abuse); social and sexual understanding (e.g. knowing the course of the development of the child's symbolic play; whether the child is aware of when it is acceptable to express and or demonstrate their knowledge of sexual relationships; moral understanding (e.g. knowing about trust; sharing information; truth).

Also needing to be included in the planning process is an assessment of the child's emotional responses to the abuse or neglect, and the possibility of disturbed thinking and behaviour occurring as a consequence of the interview. It is also necessary to be aware of the child's understanding, their use of time, and also whether any physical disability might impede the child's performance. It is easy to appreciate how the translation of the psychological principles of this approach — contextualizing the child's personal and social circumstances, and constructing a framework of apposite factors from child developmental psychology — can be undertaken for other situations. These could include, for example, where parents are separating or seeking divorce; responding to the needs of those children who are to be looked after by the local authority; and ascertaining the wishes and feelings of young people in order to make informed decisions about youth justice or special needs.

*The Phased Approach*

The Memorandum of Good Practice stresses the importance of a 'phased approach' to interviewing children:

> This treats the interview as a process in which a variety of interviewing techniques are deployed in relatively discrete phases, proceeding from general and open to specific and closed forms of question. It is suggested that this approach is likely to achieve the basic aim of listening to what the child has to say, if anything, about the alleged offence. (Home Office/DOH, 1992, p.15)

There are four phases:

(i) The development of rapport:

The rapport building phase serves two functions — to help put the child at ease, and to allow the interviewer to revise any initial ideas about the child's development. The child is led into free discussion about matters relevant to age and estimated understanding and interests. There is an important need to be aware of power issues, and thus not exerting too great an authority over the child. Children often assume that, because they are being interviewed, they must have done something wrong. It is necessary for interviewers to give reassurance to children but without conveying any guilt on the part of the alleged offender. In the context of the Memorandum, interviewers are required to ensure that the child is aware of *'the need to speak the truth and of the acceptability of saying "I don't know" or "I don't understand"'* (p.16, their emphases). It is also suggested that, to promote the child to tell the interviewer the truth, something like the following is stated: *'"You can tell me anything you want. I don't want you to feel you need hold anything back. All that matters is that you don't make anything up or leave anything out."'* (p.17, their emphases)

(ii) The free narrative account:

In the free narrative account phase, the child is 'encouraged to provide *in his or her own words* and at his or her own pace an account of the relevant event(s)' (p.17, their emphases). The aim here is to obtain spontaneous information from the child and which is free from the influence of the interviewer. Whilst it is obvious that many children may find difficulty in talking about what has happened to them, gentle reassurance is usually sufficient to help most children maintain their narration. When working with younger children, because they are likely to produce less spontaneous information, it must be remembered that it is also far easier to question them inappropriately. This often happens if interviewers are unable to maintain the silent pauses which young and older children may need when thinking about what to say next. Interviewers should maintain a quiet demeanour, accept from the child what might then be repetitive or irrelevant information, and actively listen to the child's account by appropriate feedback of the child's own words.

(iii) Differing types of questioning:

(a) When interviewing children it is important to begin with open-ended questions. These are characterized by being constructed from simple sentences, free from double negatives and any other grammatical ambiguities, and devoid of any attempt to lead or pressure the child. There is a need to be aware of certain age and developmental differences at this stage: very young children often assume that other adults will know what has happened to them, just because one adult does; young children are usually less specific in their free narrative accounts; also, young children are not likely to remember earlier episodes in a pattern of abusing behaviour because of not recognizing what was happening to them. Other necessary strategies include being aware of how children interpret questions beginning with 'why' as likely to mean to them that they are guilty. Interrupting the child must be avoided, even if uncommon or indistinct words and phrases are being used. Clarification of this nature must be made at a later point in the interview when using more specific but non-leading questions (as below).

(b)  Without employing questions which allow a 'yes' or 'no' answer, and thus continuing to use open-ended questions, interviewers can proceed to gain further details following on from information provided earlier. It is at this point that the interviewer will need to be clear about the child's concept and use of time. Wherever possible, interviewers should construct their questions using elements of the child's life experiences to refer to time-located events: their birthday, school outing, a party, bed-time, etc. A sensitive probing of any inconsistencies and words and behaviours unusual for children of particular ages should be undertaken. This is especially important for professionals responsible for gaining accounts of children who may have been abused. Also, it is important to ascertain, without attributing any blame if it has not happened, whether the child has attempted to inform anyone else about what had occurred to them.

(c)  Closed questions can be used to gain specific responses about matters previously raised by the child and which remain unclear. However, care must be taken not to frame closed questions in ways which only permit a restricted form of answering. The value of the response is likely to be of dubious value and it could mean that the interviewer has led the child into that particular answer.

(d)  'A leading question is one which implies the answer or assumes facts which are likely to be in dispute' (p.20). Interviewers are reminded that responses to leading questions are unlikely to have much evidential value in criminal proceedings if they refer to central facts of the case. If seeking a 'yes' or 'no' response, it is therefore best to ensure that subsequent questions on the same matter are phrased in such a way that the child would sometimes respond 'yes' and at other times 'no' to provide an indication of their ability to differentiate between the questions.

(iv)   Interview closure

Any interview needs to be closed in a way which leaves the child feeling as relaxed as possible and with a sense that they have not failed either themselves or others in any way. If there is a summary of the interview then this should be in the child's words and not those of the interviewer. Any questions the child may have should be answered, as appropriate. Finally, the child should be warmly thanked. Importantly, they, and/or their carer, should be given a contact name and number, in case they wish to talk again with the interviewer. It is obviously important that children leave interviews thinking positively about themselves.

The power dynamics inherent in adult-child relationships provide a context in which children can quickly become disadvantaged when being interviewed. Interviewing can easily be viewed, by children as well as adults, as a process of disempowerment if specific steps are not taken to ameliorate this weakness. All professionals who undertake direct work with children know that effective communication and interviewing are only possible by first undertaking a careful assessment of children's development (especially thinking, memory and language) alongside their emotional needs (as in their responses to stress, and their coping strategies when feeling intimidated). This is a considerable demand to make of non-specialists but Steward *et al.* (1993) provide a useful summary of some straightforward advice:

Children's performance is enhanced when tasks are simplified and when a variety of supports are provided. Some of the supports may take the form of external cues, such as those provided by certain props or forms of questioning, and some may take the form of affective cues, such as whether the child can feel free to recount an event or resist suggestion. (p.27)

The responsibility of the interviewer — whether the interview takes place within a legal, medical or educational context, etc. — is to match the methods of questioning to the cognitive skills and emotional development of the child. At issue is not only the potential for interviewers misconstruing children's accounts of events but also misjudging their sense of personal worth, especially given that they are often easily frightened in interview situations. In their anxiety to please adults, children of all ages feel that their identities are threatened and can easily become suggestible, especially when presented with questions and problems about their family and personal circumstances. Importantly, if the context for interviewing is related to assessing abuse and or neglect within the family, the interviewer is easily able to be perceived by the child as someone who has been invested with authority from their parents. Thurgood (1990) suggests that, there are 'two key aspects to be considered in listening to children in statutory work. The first is to ensure that all information relevant to a child's safety, welfare and development is co-ordinated. The second is to consider who is to work directly with the child to listen to the child's wishes, feelings and experiences' (p.53). Clearly, the need for an emotionally supportive environment in which interviewing can take place is also as necessary for contexts in which children are being assessed for foster family placements, rehabilitation to the family home, and special schooling, notwithstanding criminal proceedings in the youth courts.

The Memorandum of Good Practice (see Yuille (1989) for another example, known as 'Stepwise'; or Roberts and Glasgow (1993) for a more modular approach) has been devised by a multi-disciplinary group of researchers and practitioners to promote better interviewing of children in criminal proceedings. The Memorandum describes a four-phase approach to interviewing wherein each of the phases is a set of techniques for ascertaining the child's account of events. For professionals working in a statutory context with children, the Memorandum can be usefully translated to a wide number of settings given the sound advice on developing rapport between interviewer and child, producing a range of differing question formats and on how to close the interview and leave the child feeling positive about their contribution. Formal interviews are rarely encountered by children in contexts other than disapproval and or reprimand. It is easy to imagine therefore that a majority of children will be likely to experience being interviewed as a somewhat intimidating event and certainly not one in which they will easily feel that their views are genuinely being solicited. In essence, the advice in the Memorandum fosters a sincere and believable approach which can be used positively and creatively by a range of professionals working with children.

### Emotional Trauma and Children's Memory: Some Discussion Points

Of obvious concern to all professionals is the possibility that children who have been traumatised — for example, by abuse and or neglect (Briere, 1992); psychological difficulties because of physical disability (Breslau, 1985); the impact of crime (Morgan and Zedner, 1992) or disasters (Yule and Williams, 1992) etc., are not able accurately, if at all, to remember or make sense of what happened to them, and are therefore unlikely to impart their true wishes and feelings.

For professionals working with children in statutory contexts, and reporting on those children's needs, the requirement to be aware of the processes involved in emotional denial is keenly felt. For example, increasingly in both the private (therapeutic) and the public (legal) testimony of adult survivors of child sexual abuse, the concept of repression — the unconscious forgetting of traumatic experiences — creates much controversy (Lindsay and Read, 1994; British Psychological Society, 1995). The tragic irony of the debate into this phenomenon is that there appears to be no documented scientific research which focuses on how children think and feel in the context of childhood trauma (Loftus, 1993).

Miller's clinical and theoretical discussions (e.g. 1991; 1990) locate the genesis of repression at the heart of family life, specifically as a consequence of a range of abusive parenting behaviour. The psychology of memory in the abusing family — and Miller would say this was typical of the majority of all, not just abusing, families — is inextricably linked to the implementation and manipulation of power. In the course of abusive behaviour, it is the parental imperative to the child to forget that which constitutes the context in which repression develops. It is somehow as if children are made to believe that what their parents state, and do, is love, and which they are forbidden to feel as pain. The parental lament, 'I only do it because I love you', in the act of whatever form of abuse — physical chastisement; sexual abuse; psychological maltreatment — helps construct for the child the psychological confusion of love and pain and therefore the potential for creating circumstances in which repression behaviour is manifested.

It is not uncommon for professionals, who have a court-directed or statutory responsibility to ascertain the wishes and feelings of a child, to be asked to assess the quality of parent-child interactions. These requests vary from work relating to contact and custody, to fostering and adoption, and in relation to residential care and schooling. However, what is quite surprising is that, for example, in the arena of contact meetings between children and their parents, it is still very much the adults' wishes which appear to have greater precedence over those of their children's. By this it is meant the manner in which decisions are made on the nature and the organization of contact between parents and their children (Family Rights Group, 1994). Conclusions about the frequency and duration — notwithstanding the settings, materials, and tasks — of these sessions appear in practice to be poorly planned. For example, there is little discussion with, where developmentally appropriate, the children, or any account made of behaviours which might indicate emotionally that the (usually young child, or the child with severe learning disabilities and or communication difficulties) is expressing non-verbally that they do not wish to have such meetings. Contact is one of the most likely settings in which children's repression behaviour could be manifested, given the anxieties and fears which children may have when meeting with parents who have maltreated or neglected them.

In a study of local authorities' arrangements for contact — where contact refers not just to visits, but also to telephone and written communications — James (Social Services Inspectorate/Department of Health, 1994) noted that 'contact arrangements for individual children in some families were often necessarily highly complex (and that) courts and local authorities both see contact issues as an integral part of the overall care plan for each child, rather than as issues to be decided separately' (p.3). What is missing, however, from what is generally a useful and practice-oriented survey, is a consideration of psychological factors which inform professionals about how best they might identify the emotional benefits or risks for the children who are the subjects of the contact meetings. Professionals require the means for identifying the behaviours which children could be presenting to exemplify either a conscious or unconscious denial of the emotional and psychological impact of the interactions with their parents *et al.* What would the psychological behaviours look like that constituted what was effectively repression in action in the context of contact meetings?

Little is known scientifically about the manner in which abusive events are processed by children, although Putnam (1993) presents a clinical perspective on traumatically-induced dissociative disorders in children. The possible connections between an individual's unconscious processing and the awareness of their conscious behaviour are discussed by Brewin (1988). These phenomena are explored within a context of how individuals are potentially capable of utilizing in parallel two interactive systems for processing information. This model of functioning has many important implications for child protection work, as it suggests a way of conceptualizing how some children, living in an environment of abuse, are able to maintain a sense of their self-identity. Eth and Pynoos (1985) have documented their clinical findings from working with a range of traumatised children. Children, like adults, can exemplify diverse behaviours in response to trauma. These can be as variable as the inhibition of spontaneous thought; a disruption in learning/school performance; re-experiencing the traumatic event; new fear marked by anxious preoccupations or generalized fear to previously neutral stimuli; fear of the future; acting out behaviour (either as risk-taking or aggression to others); and constricted or morbid thoughts or fantasy.

Peterson, Prout and Schwartz (1991) propose that, 'Parental response to trauma and to the child's reactions to trauma are important variables in the amelioration or exacerbation of the stress the child experiences' (p.66). Where a parent is also an abuser the child is, however, additionally traumatized in the sense of having to reframe the whole basis of their family relationships. Some children do not experience this same form of devastating bewilderment for they seek actively to avoid thinking or talking about their trauma. It becomes, in terms of communicating with the self, as if the pain is too unbearable to contemplate and that it is experienced only to be forgotten, possibly to be resolved at another time, potentially never to be consciously thought of again.

Loftus (1993) suggests that, 'Repression is one of the most haunting concepts in psychology' (p.518). In clinical material there appears to be considerable therapeutic evidence to support the notion that even young children have acquired sufficient abilities to repress their thoughts and feelings about traumatizing experiences. The work of Miller (e.g. 1990; 1991) is imbued with a range of clinical examples which show the need for children to repress, but which also illustrate the ultimately damaging power of childhood repression. It is Miller's (1990) view that, 'The life-saving function of repression in childhood is transformed in adulthood into a life-destroying force' (p.41). According to Miller, repression is, pre-eminently, the psychological means by which children deny the reality of what is happening to them within their own families.

Whilst Miller's work is rich in clinical detail, and provides absorbing reading, her accounts do not include an adequate exposition of the cognitive and developmental processes which enable children to repress abusive and other traumatic experience. Repression needs to be viewed as the mechanism by which children come to learn *not to feel*. In this way, it is possible to construct a model of learning to repress. Children have to learn to distance themselves — become dissociated — from the reality of their abuse. In some instances children will be immediately traumatized by the initial impact of their trauma. Typically, for abused children, they will have gradually evolved a sense of having become inured to a range of abusive behaviour. Often, in abusing situations, a parent or significant carer inveigles a child over the long-term into a pattern of behaviour which has as its basis a suspension of belief about what is acceptable. In their positions of power some parents are quite capable of instructing their children in how not to feel what they are experiencing, and in how to construe what they are abusively perpetrating as parents as an extension of their love and care.

Although repression has been defined in widely varying and, potentially, paradoxical ways (Baddeley, 1990), the logic and psychology of repression is that it should clearly be located as a problem of information retrieval. An individual will have had to have remembered information from traumatic experiences for this to have been repressed. Therefore, when working directly with children it is important to try to account for how information has been stored, and how and in what circumstances it is retrieved, as these are the key features of memory behaviour which underline the repression of trauma. According to Gil (1988), many children experience traumatic events at a time when they had not fully developed language skills. Memories are thus likely to be retrieved because of visual and other sensory cues. Moreover, given the sense of powerlessness that a young child undoubtedly experiences in the context of being abused, the repression of memories occurs at times of heightened emotional arousal and helplessness. It is logical therefore to consider that these memories will only be recovered when an individual re-experiences painful emotion. To protect the self against such pain is predictable and therefore mechanisms may well be developed which attempt to prevent the surfacing of the painful memories.

It is in this context, therefore, that an awareness of the psychologically-informed technique known as the Cognitive Interview (CI) is particularly apposite (Memon, Cronin, Eaves and Bull, 1993). CI techniques aim to reinstate the physical and personal context of an event about which an eyewitness report is required. Those providing the testimony are encouraged to verbalize how they felt at the time of the event, to think back and visualize the event, to consider what other sensory information might be available from remembering, for example, what smells there might have been present, or what sounds might have been heard. Other CI techniques include recounting events in reverse order and from various starting points and differing perspectives. This could mean being asked to consider different time points during the event, how perceptions differed in time, and also the perceptions of others who might have been present. Within the model of memory which is assumed in such methods it is anticipated that these techniques will gain access to an event from a range of memory retrieval paths. Repression is inextricably related to the retrieval of emotionally traumatic events. The cognitive interview research has only been used, for ethical reasons, with children in familiar rather than traumatic contexts. It is possible, however, positively to construe the use of CI techniques with children of differing ages who are reunited with their parents in contact meetings organized by the local authority.

Matters which need to be considered include the notion that, for abused or neglected children, and this could include some disabled children who are rejected by their parents, to retain a sense of self esteem they have to construct highly specific, often very idiosyncratic, cognitive and emotional strategies about the events they experience. To cope with continuing to live within an abusing or rejecting family, and not to betray the pattern of living which maintains the abusing and or hurtful behaviour, children are (and have to be) rendered powerless. In what can sometimes be a violent shift of responsibility, although frequently in more subtle ways, an abuser places the burden of secrecy for the abuse onto the child — in possibly an infinite variety of threatening ways. These threats and enticements to such secrecy represent the further and continuing abuse of power. Children are therefore forced to communicate nothing about behaviour that is felt and known to be both wrong and unwanted. Repression becomes a taught behaviour the more the power dynamics in families become distorted. For any child to feel safe enough to reflect their pain, and to state their wishes and feelings, demands considerable bravery from the child and much ingenuity from the interviewer.

The employment of CI techniques need to be very carefully undertaken and structured in line with suggestions from The Memorandum of Good Practice. It is clearly necessary for interviewers to have an awareness of the role of power dynamics, both in the child's family and the interview setting.

## Conclusions

This chapter has considered how the work of psychologists can contribute a distinct perspective to an increasingly varied number of statutory contexts in which the process of obtaining meaningful statements from and about children has become paramount. The selection of the contents for this chapter has relied upon the general understanding that all child psychologists, whether from clinical (Herbert, 1991) or educational (Wolfendale *et al.*, 1992) psychology training backgrounds, have a thorough knowledge of the nature and varying methods of assessment, of a broad range of child and adolescent behaviour and development, and of the specific settings and systems in which these behavioural, developmental and assessment factors may become the focus of their work. Also, given the recent changes to many of the laws affecting children, young people and/or their families — as in the legislation concerning child witnesses (Criminal Justice Acts, 1988, 1991); the proposed secure training centres for young offenders (Criminal Justice and Public Order Act, 1994); in the overhaul of the child care law (Children Act, 1989); and the statutes governing the assessment of children's special education needs (Education Act, 1993) — professionals have never before been in a position where they have needed a comprehensive and practice-based understanding of the range of statutory and criminological contexts to which they could apply a psychological perspective.

Psychologists' work with children is rarely bound by having to perform statutory duties. Child psychologists have several legal responsibilities, but these — variously concerned with issues of consent; having regard to the notion of a 'duty of care'; confidentiality; and not making false claims about professional expertise — are the same for all professionals working with children, irrespective of their particular discipline. Educational psychologists who are employed directly by local education authorities do have a statutory duty to undertake the assessment of children's special education needs (Education Act, 1993). However, as Conn (1992) states: 'It is not usually the Education Acts which cause the most psychologically complex issues to emerge and which create the greatest difficulty in marrying psychological and legal concepts' (p.154). Some educational psychologists might disagree with this view, given that more appeals about certain children's special educational needs — notably relating to dyslexia and the provision of specialist educational placements and therapies — are increasingly being taken to tribunals. However, whilst the seeking of children's views is rarely as contentious in this arena as it can be in social care and youth offending contexts, listening to the views of children with special educational needs is a relatively new phenomenon. Furthermore, special educational needs children (even those being formally assessed) have at present no right to have their views taken into account.

The Children Act 1989 sets new legal standards in relation to 'ascertaining the wishes and feelings of children' in that, as Bainham (1990) identifies, the Act 'has unquestionably shifted this towards a greater degree of involvement in decision-making for children. It is perhaps at least psychologically significant that children's views appear at the top of the statutory checklist' (p.14). These changes in child and family law have consequently meant that the delivery of children's psychology services — from whatever professional setting — have had, and will have in ways yet to evolve, to be modified into being more overtly shaped by the demands of child advocacy and based on the emergent professional and research interests in family psychology (Liddle, 1987), forensic child psychology (Roberts and Glasgow, 1993) and anti-discriminatory practice which, for the first time, is legally enforced for children looked after by the local authority, as stated in the Children Act (1989) s 22 (5). It is in this manner, therefore, that applied psychologists have an overriding responsibility for ensuring that the child's voice is heard within the context of the dynamics and interactions of their family and the law. It is not surprising to find that the most significant element of recent reforms to child and family law (whether relating to schooling, child care, or youth offending) has centred upon the responsibilities of parents towards their children, and about how parents might work in partnership with statutory and voluntary services in attempting to meet their children's needs. A psychological perspective is able to offer a framework within which it is possible to assess the difficulties that exist for children relating their experiences about events: if they are not elicited sensitively, and within a pre-planned structure, this could mean the facilitation of views which are not adequately representative of the child's wishes and feelings.

## References

BADDELEY, A. (1990) *Human Memory: Theory and Practice*, Hove, Lawrence Erlbaum Associates.

BAINHAM, A. (1990) *Children: The New Law: The Children Act 1989*, Bristol, Family Law.

BRESLAU, N. (1985) 'Psychiatric disorder in children with physical disabilities', *Journal of the American Academy of Child Psychiatry*, **24**, pp.87–94.

BREWIN, C. (1988) *Cognitive Foundations of Clinical Psychology*, Hove, Lawrence Erlbaum Associates.

BRIERE, J.N. (1992) *Child Abuse Trauma: Theory and Treatment of the Lasting Effects*, Newbury Park, CA, Sage Publications.

BRITISH PSYCHOLOGICAL SOCIETY (1995) *Recovered Memories*, Leicester, BPS Publications.

BUTLER-SLOSS, E. (1988) *Report of the Inquiry into Child Abuse in Cleveland 1987*, London, Her Majesty's Stationery Office.

CECI, S.J. (1994) 'Psychology in litigation and legislation', in SALES, B.D. and VANDENBOS, G.R. (Eds) *The Master Lectures*, Washington, DC, American Psychological Association.

CECI, S.J. and BRUCK, M. (1993) 'The suggestibility of the child witness: A historical review and synthesis', *Psychological Bulletin*, **113**, pp.403–39.

CECI, S.J., ROSS, D.F. and TOGLIA, M.P. (Eds) (1989) *Perspectives in Children's Testimony*, New York, Springer-Verlag.

CLYDE, J. (1992) *The Report of the Inquiry into the Removal of Children from Orkney in February 1991*, Edinburgh, Her Majesty's Stationery Office.

CONN, W. (1992) 'Psychologists, child law and the courts: contexts and professional advice', in WOLFENDALE, S., BRYANS, T., FOX, M., LABRAM, A. and SIGSTON, A. (Eds) *The Profession and Practice of Educational Psychology: Future Directions*, London, Cassell.

DAVIE, R. (1993) 'The psychologist as expert witness in children's cases', *Family Law*, February, pp.52–53.

DAVIES, G.M. (1995) 'Sex, lies and videotapes', Unpublished paper presented to a Scientific Meeting of the British Agencies for Adoption and Fostering, Coleshill.

DAVIES, G.M. (1994) 'Children's testimony: Research findings and policy implications', *Psychology, Crime and Law*, **1**, pp.175–80.

DENT, H. and FLIN, R. (Eds) (1992) *Children as Witnesses*, Chichester, Wiley.

ETH, S. and PYNOOS, R.S. (1985) *Post-Traumatic Stress Disorder in Children*, Washington, American Psychiatric Press.

EVANS, G. and WEBB, M. (1993) 'High profile — but not that high profile: interviewing of young persons', *Issues in Criminological and Legal Psychology*, **18**, pp.37–45.

FAMILY RIGHTS GROUP (1994) *Contact with Children Looked After by the Local Authority*, London, Family Rights Group.

GIL, E. (1988) *Treatment of Adult Survivors of Childhood Abuse*, Walnut Creek, CA, Launch Press.

GOODMAN, G.S., RUDY, L., BOTTOMS, B. and AMAN, C. (1990) 'Children's concerns and memory: Issues of ecological validity in the study of children's eyewitness testimony', in FIVUSH, R. and HUDSON, J. (Eds) *Knowing and Remembering in Young Children*, New York, Cambridge University Press.

HEIMAN, M.L. (1992) 'Annotation: putting the puzzle together: validating allegations of child sexual abuse', *Journal of Child Psychology and Psychiatry*, **33**, 2, pp.311–29.

HERBERT, M. (1991) *Clinical Child Psychology: Social Learning, Development and Behaviour*, London, Wiley.

HOME OFFICE/DEPARTMENT OF HEALTH (1992) *Memorandum of Good Practice: On Video Recorded Interviews with Child Witnesses for Criminal Proceedings*, London, Her Majesty's Stationery Office.

JOHNSON, K. (1989) *Trauma in the Lives of Children*, Basingstoke, Macmillan.

JONES, D.P.H. (1993) *Interviewing the Sexually Abused Child: Investigation of Suspected Abuse*, London, Gaskell.

LIDDLE, H.A. (1987) 'Family psychology: the Journal, the field', *Journal of Family Psychology*, **1**, 1, pp.5–22.

LINDSAY, D.S. and READ, J.D. (1994) 'Psychotherapy and memories of childhood sexual abuse: A cognitive perspective', *Applied Cognitive Psychology*, **8**, 4, pp.281–338.

LOFTUS, E. (1993) 'The reality of repressed memories', *American Psychologist*, **48**, 5, pp.518–37.

MEMON, A., CRONIN, O., EAVES, R. and BULL, R. (1993) 'The cognitive interview and child witnesses', *Issues in Criminological and Legal Psychology*, **20**, pp.3–9.

MILLER, A. (1991) *Breaking Down the Wall of Silence: To Join the Waiting Child*, London, Virago.

MILLER, A. (1990) *Banished Knowledge: Facing Childhood Injuries*, London, Virago.

MORGAN, J. and ZEDNER, L. (1992) *Child Victims: Crime, Impact, and Criminal Justice*, Oxford, Clarendon Press.

MORTON, J. (1988) 'When can lying start?', *Issues in Criminological and Legal Psychology*, **13**, pp.35–36.

ORNSTEIN, P.A. (1991) 'Putting interviewing in context', in DORIS, J. (Ed) *The Suggestibility of Children's Recollections: Implications for Eyewitness Testimony*, Washington, DC, American Psychological Association.

PETERSON, K.C., PROUT, M.F. and SCHWARTZ, R.A. (1991) *Post-Traumatic Stress Disorder: A Clinician's Guide*, New York, Plenum Press.

PUTNAM, F.W. (1993) 'Dissociative disorders in children: Behavioral profiles and problems', *Child Abuse and Neglect*, **17**, pp.39–45.

ROBERTS, H. and GLASGOW, D. (1993) 'Gathering evidence from children: A systematic approach', *Issues in Criminological and Legal Psychology*, **20**, pp.10–14.

SOCIAL SERVICES INSPECTORATE/DEPARTMENT OF HEALTH (1994) *The Children Act 1989: Contact Orders Study: A Study of Local Authority Decision Making Around Contact Applications Under Section 34*, London, Department of Health.

SPENCER, J. and FLIN, R. (1990) *The Evidence of Children, The Law and The Psychology*, London, Blackstone.

STEIN, N.L. and JEWETT, J.L. (1986) 'A conceptual analysis of the meaning of negative emotions', in IZARD, C.E. and READ, P.B. (Eds) *Measuring Emotions in Infants and Children, Vol 2,* Cambridge, Cambridge University Press.

STEPHENSON, G.M. (1992) *The Psychology of Criminal Justice,* Oxford, Blackwell.

STEWARD, M., BUSSEY, K., GOODMAN, G., and SAYWITZ, K. (1993) 'Implications of developmental research for interviewing children', *Child Abuse and Neglect,* **17,** pp.25–37.

THURGOOD, J. (1990) 'Active listening — a social services perspective', in BANNISTER, A., BARRETT, K. and SHEARER, E. (Eds) *Listening to Children: The Professional Response to Hearing the Abused Child,* Harlow, Longman.

WOLFENDALE, S., BRYANS, T., FOX, M., LABRAM, A. and SIGSTON, A. (Eds) (1992) *The Profession and Practice of Educational Psychology: Future Directions,* London, Cassell.

YUILLE, J. (1989) *Text Credibility Assessment,* Boston, Kluwer Academic Publishers.

YULE, W. and WILLIAMS, R.M. (1992) 'The management of trauma following disasters', in LANE, D.A. and MILLER, A. (Eds) *Child and Adolescent Therapy: A Handbook,* Buckingham, Open University Press.

# 5 The Voice of the Child in Mental Health Practice

*Danya Glaser*

In discussing the child's voice within mental health practice, three aspects need to be considered, namely the context, content and status of the voice. In recent times, much of the discussion has centred around the question of the status of the child's voice, attention being drawn to those cases where a child, or more commonly an adolescent, has refused treatment. Several such cases have led to public debate, having gained publicity in the media. These are indeed important cases, which call for clarification of principles and practice. They do, however, concern only one aspect of the child's voice and only a minority of those young persons who are referred to, and receive, child mental health services. In this chapter, these three aspects of the child's voice and their interrelationship will be considered.

## Context

Children rarely initiate their own attendance at child psychiatric, child guidance or child mental health settings. They are unlikely to know that what concerns adults about them or the emotional discomfort which they might experience, can be defined as a symptom and is amenable to treatment. Whilst children are familiar with doctors, hospitals and the practice of medicine, they are unlikely to have heard of child psychiatrists, psychologists, psychotherapists and other professionals in the mental health field. Not infrequently, children and young persons attending these services for the first time are unsure why they have come, let alone what to expect. It is in this context that the notion of the child's voice needs to be considered.

Being unaware of its existence and function, the child is unable to request psychological or psychiatric help. Once there, the inevitable sense of disempowerment which all patients feel to a greater or lesser extent is compounded for the child. Young children are structurally dependent, older children and adolescents socially dependent on their care-giving adults. Children's relative powerlessness is therefore both understandable and possibly at times very appropriate. Whatever its merits or deficiencies, this relative absence of a voice requires explicit recognition. George Bernard Shaw's remark that 'all professions are conspiracies against the laity' (Shaw, 1947, p.106) applies in double measure to children attending child mental health services.

### Relationships

Implicit in a young person's consultation with mental health services is a triangular system of relationships:

Each of the three will have different knowledge, wishes, expectations, concerns and feelings which will influence the resultant interaction (Pearce, 1994). The child's, parents' and professional's voices do not, however, carry equal weight and are not equally articulated, heard or acknowledged. Nor are their positions necessarily independent of each other's. In particular, the child's psychiatric disorder may well be causally related to the parent–child interaction.

The aim of the child psychiatric work includes alleviating the distress of the child, reducing concerns about the child's behaviour or well-being and improving the relationships between the child and his or her family and peers. There is a quest for new, joint understandings. In the process, there may at times be a lack of consensus, or differences and disagreement may arise. The alignment of agreements and differences will vary from case to case. There may be situations where child, parent and professional each hold different viewpoints. More often, there is a measure of agreement between two of the protagonists. The nature of the alignment is of considerable significance for the child. If, for example, the child's viewpoint is acknowledged by neither parent nor professional, the child will feel both very isolated and powerless and unless independently represented may, indeed, remain so. An example of such a situation was reported by Graham and Foreman (1995), concerning an eight year old girl who presented with a pervasive refusal syndrome (Lask *et al.*, 1991). Following hospitalization and gradual recovery, she refused to return home, resisting the wishes of both her parents and the treating clinicians. In other cases, the child and parents may together disagree with an opinion or proposal put forward by a clinician. Although from the latter's point of view the child may then be in a very vulnerable position, the young person continues to experience an alliance with his parent(s) or primary carers. By contrast, the comfort which the child might derive from being supported by a professional in a situation of conflict between the child and the parents is vitiated by the child's distress at the fact of the conflict. This is important because rarely does a child come to feel entirely free from his or her primary caregivers, whatever their capacity to meet his or her needs.

79

*Clinical Settings*

Another aspect of context is the setting within which the interaction between child and family, and the mental health service takes place. Most work is in out-patient settings, often involving several family members. Invariably, much of the conversation is ABOUT the child, particularly when the concerns centre on the child's behaviour. This is often very appropriate and may well be born out of concern for the child's welfare. What may be inadvertently omitted is not so much the child's version of events; rather, there is not always an acknowledgment of the child's experience of being the subject of the conversation.

The use of one-way screens and video recordings in the course of thera-peutic work has allowed for creative innovation in work with troubled children and their families (Burnham, 1986). The degree to which children are consulted about the use of these facilities varies as does the degree to which their response influences practice.

In clinical practice, there is a degree of choice to be made between differ-ent therapeutic settings, modalities and sometimes therapeutic goals. Although not mutually exclusive, there are individual, group or family settings; a predom-inantly behavioural, psychodynamic, family systems or psychopharmacological orientation (Jacobs, 1993); and different desired outcomes being sought (Marcus and Schopler, 1994). The route selected is determined in part by clinical indi-cations. In addition, both professional and parental preferences contribute to the decision. The child's preference is elicited less often, possibly because it is considered to be insufficiently informed. A particular instance is a child who is refusing to attend school for reasons of phobic anxiety and for whom the appropriate treatment might include a degree of coercion in the therapeutic effort to overcome the anxiety (Jones, 1991).

The admission of children and adolescents to in-patient units presents a very different context for the child's voice to be heard. This includes both the decision-making process about admission and the child's voice as an in-patient.

*Research*

Some clinical interventions in child psychiatric practice are offered within con-trolled trials which might include a variety of therapeutic modalities or drugs (e.g. Remschmidt, 1994). The maintenance of good clinical practice is also reliant on research which yields baseline data and follow-up information (Klin and Cohen, 1994). Much of the data gathered in such research are of no benefit to the particular child/respondent. A fourth party is thus introduced into the triangular relationship between child, parent and professional/researcher. This is the (anonymous) future beneficiary of the results obtained from the research. In order to give informed consent to research, the child needs to be made aware of this potential beneficiary.

There has been considerable debate about the child's voice in research settings in terms of validity of consent and the child's right to be consulted (Laor, 1994). Situations have arisen, where adults, in their wish to protect children from possible trauma, have declined to consult children about their participation in research. An instance was a follow-up study of children who had been sexually abused. The aim of this study was to seek the children's views about the professional involvement and treatment which they had received as well as to assess their mental health. Children were thus denied the choice of contributing to a study in which their voice was actively sought and in which they could have benefited other children (Prior *et al.*, 1994).

## Content

Within a doctor-patient or professional-client relationship, one might conceptualize the 'recipient's' position to be placed somewhere along a continuum of:

*Being compelled — refusal — objection — misgivings — questions — submission — implicit consent — active consent.*

When an adult patient consults a doctor there is in that interaction, subject to adequate explanation, implicit consent to being examined, having investigations carried out and accepting the advice given. The latter might include ingestion of medication or receiving some form of therapy. This implicit consent is predicated on the possession of information. Without the possession of information and the acquisition of explanation, implicit consent cannot be considered valid. Active, written consent is only required for invasive procedures or those under anaesthesia.

The same cannot be said to apply to children, even when they have acquired sufficient language to understand age-appropriate explanations. Although, as is more commonly the practice in child mental health, efforts are made to involve the child through explanations, it is arguable to what extent the question of consequent consent by the child is of primary concern and actually sought. And yet the child may well, if invited, have misgivings or objections to voice. Children are only likely to exercise their voice spontaneously at the negative extreme of the continuum and be invited only at the positive end. However, most interactions in child mental health will, in practice, take place within the middle range where, unless actively sought, the child's voice will not be heard. Although the child's silence in this area does not violate his or her legal rights, good practice which includes enhancing the likelihood of a better outcome, should encourage clinicians to enable children to express their worries, opinions and questions. Article 12 of the UN Convention of the Rights of the Child (1989) states that

> States parties shall assure to the child, who is capable of forming his or her own views, the right to express those views freely in all matters

affecting the child, the views of the child being given due weight in accordance with the age and maturity of the child.

The Convention has not been incorporated into UK law and does not therefore currently carry any legal authority.

From the child's point of view, a consultation may carry the meaning of blame and attribution of badness or failure. A young person may feel ashamed at the relatively public exposition of his or her shortcomings or weaknesses, when a child's anxieties are being discussed. The therapeutic process may well be appropriate, although what may be missing is the open and sensitive exploration, subsequent recognition and acknowledgment of the child's position within the process. The child may well also have unanswered, and sometimes unarticulated, questions about the consultation. Unless actively sought, they may not emerge.

### Confidentiality

A particular aspect is the child's possible wish for confidentiality or privacy. This may concern specific aspects of information about the child or the child may wish information to be withheld from particular persons, for instance certain family members and, not infrequently, teachers. Within child psychiatric practice, there are occasions when reports about the child are required for referral or legal purposes. It is necessary and appropriate to discuss the contents of the report with the child prior to its release. The wish for confidentiality may be well founded. Alternatively, the child may have unnecessary misgivings about the consequences of certain persons' knowledge about the child's difficulties. It is only possible to assess the extent to which it is in the child's best interests to honour confidentiality, after exploring the child's concerns.

It is not always possible to accede to the wishes to maintain confidentiality, nor is it always in the child's best interests so to do. This is particularly so when child abuse or a serious crime are at issue. However, when confidentiality is breached, the reason for this and the course to be taken should always be fully discussed with the child first.

### Status

The status of the child's voice is of very major significance. It informs the extent to which it is necessary to heed the child's voice from an ethical and legal point of view. As already discussed, good practice would dictate that the child's voice should be heard regardless of the need for explicit consent. Those particular situations in which consent is required raise the question of the child's eligibility to give or withhold that consent. The issue of giving consent rests on questions of a child's autonomy, capacity for self determination and competence.

The minority and voiceless status of children has been based on society's more or less explicit wish to protect their welfare and on the recognition of their immaturity. This approach has been promoted to ensure the best interests of the child. Eekelaar (1994) cautions against the assumption that preservation of a status within society necessarily serves the interests of the status holder. He quotes Graveson (1953, p.13) who describes 'the origins of legal status as being a means of preserving the existing social order'. Eekelaar also questions the validity of the assumptions underpinning the 'best interests' principle. The desirability of according special recognition to children is not in dispute. It is the nature and validity of the assumptions attached to childhood and the question of how to reconcile these assumptions with the need to accord rights to the child which are at issue.

'Best interests' are socially determined and will therefore vary between different societies. Eekelaar introduces the notion of 'dynamic self-determinism'. He describes the process whereby the secure, developing child is constantly exposed to a range of environmental experiences and influences from which he or she learns. As the child matures, she or he is encouraged to draw on these influences and progressively contribute in increasing measure to decisions affecting the child. The child participates in the shaping of his or her destiny which is more likely, therefore, to meet the child's best interests. Decision-making is not, however, delegated to the child.

The development of children's logical thought processes has been schematically documented by Piaget (Piaget and Inhelder, 1958) with a progression from pre-operational, through concrete operational to formal operational thought. The ages at which children are believed to attain these cognitive developmental stages are likely to be lower and more variable than those originally suggested by Piaget. However, the nature of the progression has been established. In relation to psychiatric treatment, this process has been reported in a study by Weithorn and Campbell (1982) of children's decision-making. While nine year olds were able to express clear preferences for some treatments, they experienced some difficulties in evaluating all the factors involved. Fourteen year olds performed comparably to adults.

The status of the child's voice is clearly related to the perceived competence of the child. Competence relies on the possession of information and the capacity to process this information in particular ways. In relation to treatment or research, the information must include the nature and purpose of the proposed procedures, the attendant benefits, risks and side effects and the consequences of not participating. Alderson (1993) has convincingly shown that even children younger than ten who had been prepared in an age-appropriate manner, were able to give informed consent to orthopaedic surgery.

In order to be regarded as competent, the person also has to be autonomous. Autonomy implies that the individual feels free to make his or her own choice. It includes the liberty to choose to make or not make a decision, or to nominate someone to make the decision on one's behalf. Raz (1986) considers that the goals towards which choices are made are also relevant to autonomy.

He states that the goals of an autonomous person must be achievable within the person's social context. Furthermore, he confirms the truism that 'the completely autonomous person is an impossibility' (p.155). Given that children are dependent beings, at least emotionally and socially, they are bound and indeed expected to be influenced by, particularly, their parents, carers and teachers and later, peers. The child's secure attachment (Bowlby, 1977) to their carer requires cognitive and emotional consonance between the two. As Eekelaar (1994:57) points out, it is therefore to be expected that adults, and the more so children, will be naturally influenced by their upbringing and this should not in itself render a child incompetent by reason of relative lack of autonomy.

Principle I of the Nurenberg Code (1949:181) laid the foundation for subsequent definitions of consent. It required that consent be voluntary, that the person should have legal capacity to give consent, should be able to exercise free power of choice without being subject to coercion or constraint and should have sufficient knowledge and comprehension of the relevant subject matter. More recently, consent in the UK has been defined as 'the voluntary and continuing permission of the patient to receive a particular treatment, based on an adequate knowledge of the purpose, nature, likely effects and risks of that treatment, including the likelihood of its success and any alternatives to it' (Department of Health and Welsh Office, 1990, para 15). For consent thus defined to be valid, it therefore needs to be fully informed and freely given. In order to be eligible to consent, a child would be required to be of sufficient emotional maturity, intelligence and understanding in relation to the particular issues involved in the consent (Jones, 1991), as well as being capable from a mental health perspective.

Freeman (1993) refers to Lord Donaldson's distinction between the right to consent and the right to determine whether treatment will take place, i.e. the possession of a veto. Others have drawn a useful distinction between the child's assent and a parent's permission, pointing out that neither are, by themselves, sufficient but both are necessary (Levine, 1991).

## Legal Issues

The situation regarding children's consent to, and refusal of, psychiatric treatment is complex. A recent publication by the Children's Legal Centre outlines the current position (Harbour and Ayotte, 1995).

### Consent

According to the Code of Practice 1993 to the Mental Health Act, 1983 (Department of Health and Welsh Office, 1993), a child who has 'sufficient understanding and intelligence' can make decisions about her or his treatment in the same way as an adult. Thus, a child who is willing to be admitted to hospital could be so, even in the face of parental objection. The parents could however have recourse to the law. Any young person aged sixteen to seventeen who is 'capable of expressing his own wishes' can admit or discharge him or herself informally, irrespective of parental wishes.

### Refusal

The status of a young person's refusal is less clear. A parent or guardian does not have the right to have a child admitted to hospital informally against the child's will, provided a doctor considers that the child has the capacity to make such a decision (Department of Health and Welsh Office, 1993). In an emergency, treatment for a disturbed child of any age who is refusing treatment, is legally permissible if consent by a parent is given (Re K, W and H 1993:854 and 1994:162). In the absence of consent by parent or child, urgent treatment of such a child could be administered under common law in order to prevent a serious and immediate danger to the patient or other people, providing the treatment is reasonable and is confined to the termination of the emergency.

It has been suggested (McCall-Smith, 1992) that to refuse permission for treatment is a higher order activity than to consent. Indeed, in the UK, the withholding of consent is subject to criteria extending beyond competence (Devereux, Jones and Dickenson, 1993). This situation has arisen following two judgments in the House of Lords (Re R 1991:592; Re: W 1992:758). The cases concerned two young persons aged fifteen and sixteen respectively, who had withheld consent to psychiatric treatment. Despite both girls being deemed 'Gillick competent', that is 'of sufficient understanding to make an informed decision' (Gillick, 1986), it was considered that the court's inherent jurisdiction could override the wishes of a child, in the best interests of that child. There have been three further cases of children refusing treatment who have been overruled by the courts under the Children Act (Re K, W and H 1993:854 and 1994:162; Re E 1993:386; South Glamorgan, 1993).

It is possible for even a competent seventeen year olds refusal to be overruled by those with parental responsibility (that is parents or the local authority), by the courts (Pearce, 1994) or by recourse to the Mental Health Act 1983. There has been debate about selecting the appropriate course and agency to overrule the child in a situation of a child's refusal to be treated or admitted to a psychiatric unit. The factors to be considered are:

(i) the child's age and maturity and
(ii) the relative merits of using, respectively, the Children Act or the Mental Health Act.

Although competency or capacity can only be very approximately related to a specific age there is, in practice, a tendency to assume that a child under the age of fourteen is more appropriately considered to require the responsible protection of parental authority. This is arguable since it is possible that younger children could, in fact, be shown to be Gillick competent (e.g. Alderson, 1993). Parental permission or consent has, for instance, been accepted (in the author's personal experience) as capable of overruling a twelve year old's objection to treatment. This occurred even though this objection was only being voiced by the young person at the time when she was clearly psychologically disordered. There was good evidence to indicate that at other times, this young person would have been regarded as 'of sufficient understanding to make an informed decision' (Gillick, 1986). It could be argued that, other than in an emergency, the child who is refusing treatment because of their disordered mental state (rather than on the basis of immaturity and insufficient understanding) should receive treatment under the Mental Health Act in the same way as a mentally disordered adult would. Section 2 refers to persons 'suffering from a mental disorder which is linked to a risk to their own health or safety, or the need to protect others'. There is no minimum age limit for treatment under the Mental Health Act (Department of Health and Welsh Office, 1993). It is important to note that patients detained under the Mental Health Act may only be treated against their wishes for their 'mental disorder'. Consent is still required for treatment of other conditions except in an emergency.

Paradoxically, the use of the Mental Health Act to detain and treat a young person suffering from a mental disorder would signal an expression of respect for that young person's maturity. It can also become increasingly distressing for, and impose an unreasonable burden on, a parent to be required to consent to treatment for their disturbed child and the Mental Health Act offers a means of resolving this predicament.

Elton *et al.* (1995), however, contend that if it is deemed necessary to turn to the law in overruling the child rather than to rely on parental permission when the child objects, it is then preferable to use the Children Act rather than the Mental Health Act. Whilst preferring the Children Act, they point out some advantages of the Mental Health Act which recognize the child's competence, allow for much speedier resolution of the question of treatment, include recourse to an independent second opinion and are much less costly. Nevertheless, despite the fact that use of the Children Act may well lead to wardship or the inherent jurisdiction of the court with implications of diminished freedom for the duration of the child's minority, what is being avoided is imposing the stigma of having been sectioned under the Mental Health Act. This latter carries risks of long term stigmatization affecting situations such as obtaining a visa and insurance. Furthermore, under Children Act proceedings, the child is accorded a full voice and the possibility of independent representation.

Under the Children Act (1989) a child may be subject to, among others, an emergency protection order, an interim care or supervision order, a supervision order or a child assessment order. Psychiatric examinations within these orders would normally require the consent of the child, provided she or he has the capacity to consent. However, again the child's refusal is liable to being overruled by invoking the court's inherent jurisdiction or by using wardship.

Dealing with a child's refusal to consent differently from the giving of consent, has been regarded as a contravention of the spirit of the Children Act (1989) by several commentators including Freeman (1993), who states that 'if we denigrate and undermine (adolescents) we cannot expect responsibility in return' (p.19). In its concern to include children in decisions affecting their lives, the Children Act states as the first item in the welfare checklist that due account should be accorded to 'the ascertainable wishes and feelings of the child considered in the light of his age and understanding'. Diminishing the authority of the child's refusal could also be regarded as weakening the significance of the child's right to consent.

### Informal Admission

Concern has been expressed about the informal admission of young persons to psychiatric units, following consent by their parents or those otherwise legally responsible for them (Mental Health Act Commission, 1993). It is suggested that such an admission might constitute a 'de facto' detention (Harbour and Ayotte, 1995) unless the young person's consent has been obtained explicitly, if she or he is 'Gillick competent'. Indeed, the 1993 Mental Health Act Code of Practice (Department of Health and Welsh Office, 1993, para 30.5) reiterates the need to gain the consent to admission of any young person who has the capacity to make such a decision. Particular difficulty may arise if, during an informal admission, a need arises to restrain the young person by definition, against his or her wishes. The relative merits and disadvantages of two possible courses of action need to be evaluated: there is the possibility of detaining the young person under the Mental Health Act with the attendant risks already mentioned. It is also possible to seek secure accommodation under the Children Act. Jones (1991) cautioned against this possibility arising, particularly following guidance and regulations regarding the degree of restraint which may be applied to children in hospital under Section 25 of the Children Act (1989) (Department of Health, 1991: para 1.91(iv), Chapter 8 and Annex G).

### Conclusions — Good Practice

New terms have been introduced into the field of health service provision, one of which is 'user empowerment'. The elicitation of the child's voice is one aspect of user empowerment. Clarity is, however, required if false expectations are not to be raised for the child. As has been discussed, the act of seeking the child's voice cannot always lead to the fulfilment of the child's wishes. There is a gradation from expression of feelings and wishes, to involvement, participation and decision. Whatever the child's age and ability, a mental health professional who meets with a child might be expected to gain an awareness of the child's views and be able to communicate this awareness to the child so as to enable the child to feel heard and validated. Furthermore, the child is entitled to a clear explanation of the status of their involvement. In much of clinical practice, the child can participate in the determination of the status of his or her involvement. The child may or may not wish to participate in or make decisions, and has the right not to be burdened with the responsibilities which decisions carry.

Because child psychiatric practice includes few procedures and consists, in the main, of conversations and play, the need for informal consent is far less apparent. This is in contrast to the practice of other branches of medicine where the frequent need to make physical contact with the patient obliges the doctor to explain her or his actions and ask for the patient's permission as a matter of course.

Good practice also includes ensuring that the child is fully informed. Much of the underestimation of children's capacity to understand and therefore consent is due to the age-inappropriate language which is often used in communication with them. Their immaturity is related less to a difficulty in the grasping of concepts or in power of reasoning; they do, however, lack linguistic sophistication and life experience. Both the latter can be addressed to a significant extent, respectively through the use of simple, jargon-free language and by explaining consequences which the child would not be able to foresee.

As Pearce (1994) argues, the majority of children wish to be consulted and to receive explanations but seek to remain in accord with their parents whom they wish to trust. Children are more often troubled by discord between the significant adults around them than by their own impulse to contradict or disagree with them. Finally, there are times when a child may wish not to know certain facts which may include details of disturbing events and experiences. Respecting the child's wishes may not, in the longer term, meet his or her best interests, but hearing the child's voice will allow for an exploration of the child's reluctance.

## References

ALDERSON, P. (1993) *Children's Consent to Surgery*, Milton Keynes, Open University Press.

BOWLBY, J. (1977) 'The making and breaking of affectional bonds', *British Journal of Psychiatry*, **130**, pp.201–10.

BURNHAM, J. (1986) *Family Therapy*, London, Tavistock Publications.

DEPARTMENT OF HEALTH (1991) *The Children Act 1989: Guidance and Regulations: Vol 4, Residential Care*, London, HMSO.

DEPARTMENT OF HEALTH AND WELSH OFFICE (1990) *Code of Practice, Mental Health Act, 1983*, London, HMSO.

DEPARTMENT OF HEALTH AND WELSH OFFICE (1993) *Code of Practice, Mental Health Act, 1983*, London, HMSO.

DEVEREUX, J.A., JONES, D.P.H. and DICKENSON, D.L. (1993) 'Can children withhold consent to treatment?' *British Medical Journal*, **306**, pp.1459–1461.

EEKELAAR, J. (1994) 'The interests of the child and the child's wishes: The role of dynamic self-determinism', in ALSTON, P. (Ed) *The Best Interests of the Child*, Oxford, Clarendon Press.

ELTON, A., HONIG, P., BENTOVIM, A. and SIMONS, J. (1995) 'Withholding consent to lifesaving treatment: Three cases', *British Medical Journal*, **310**, pp.373–77.

FREEMAN, M. (1993) Removing rights from adolescents, *Adoption and Fostering*, **17**, pp.14–21.

GILLICK V WEST NORFOLK AND WISBECH AREA HEALTH AUTHORITY (1986) 1 CA 112–207.

GRAHAM, P.J. and FOREMAN, D.M. (1995) 'An ethical dilemma in child and adolescent psychiatry', *Psychiatric Bulletin*, **19**, pp.84–6.

GRAVESON, R. (1953) *Status in the Common Law*, University of London Legal Series No. 2, London, Athlone Press.

HARBOUR, A. and AYOTTE, W. (1995) *Mental Health Handbook*, London, Children's Legal Centre.

JACOBS, B. (1993) 'Treatment in child and adolescent psychiatry', in BLACK, D. and COTTRELL, D. (Eds) *Seminars in Child and Adolescent Psychiatry*, London, Gaskell.

JONES, D.P.H. (1991) 'Working with the children act: Tasks and responsibilities of the child and adolescent psychiatrist', in *Proceedings of the Children Act 1989 Course*, Occasional Paper OP12, London, The Royal College of Psychiatrists.

KLIN, A. and COHEN, D. (1994) 'The immorality of not-knowing: The ethical imperative to conduct research in child and adolescent psychiatry', in HATTAB, J. (Ed) *Ethics and Child Mental Health*, Jerusalem, Gefen.

LAOR, N. (1994) Toward liberal guidelines for clinical research with children, in HATTAB, J. (Ed) *Ethics and Child Mental Health*, Jerusalem, Gefen.

LASK, B., BRITTEN, C., KROLL, L., MAGAGNA, J. and TRANTER, M. (1991) 'Children with pervasive refusal', *Archives of Diseases in Childhood*, **66**, pp.866–69.

LEVINE, R. (1991) 'Respect for children as research subjects', in LEWIS, M. (Ed) *Child and Adolescent Psychiatry*, Baltimore, Williams and Wilkins.

McCALL-SMITH, I. (1992) 'Consent to treatment in childhood', *Archives of Diseases in Childhood*, **67**, pp.1247–1248.

MARCUS, L. and SCHOPLER, E. (1994) 'Ethics and behaviour therapy with children', in HATTAB, J. (Ed) *Ethics and Child Mental Health*, Jerusalem, Gefen.

MENTAL HEALTH ACT COMMISSION (1993) *The Fifth Biennial Report*, London, HMSO.

NURENBERG CODE (1949) in *Trials of War Criminals before the Nurenberg Military Tribunals*. Control Council Law no. 10. (vol. 2), Washington, US Government Printing Office.

PEARCE, J. (1994) 'Consent to treatment during childhood', *British Journal of Psychiatry*, **165**, pp.713–16.

PIAGET, J. and INHELDER, B. (1958) *The Growth of Logical Thinking from Childhood to Adolescence*, New York, Basic Books.

PRIOR, V., GLASER, D. and LYNCH, M. (1994) 'Child sexual abuse follow up research: ethical issues', Paper presented at Second Association for Child Psychology and Psychiatry European Conference 'Interfaces: Working with Others', Winchester, UK.

RAZ, J. (1986) *The Morality of Freedom*, Oxford, Oxford University Press.

RE E (1993) 1 Family Law Reports 386.

RE K, W and H (1993) *1 Family Law Reports 854 and (1994) 1 Family Law Reports 162*.

RE R (1991) *Weekly Law Reports 3*, pp.592–608.

RE W (1992) *Weekly Law Reports 3*, pp.758–82.

REMSCHMIDT, H. (1994) 'Ethical aspects and treatment in child psychiatry', in HATTAB, J. (Ed) *Ethics and Child Mental Health*, Jerusalem, Gefen.

SHAW, B. (1947) *The Doctor's Dilemma*, London, Constable and Company.

SOUTH GLAMORGAN COUNTY COUNCIL v W AND B (1993) *1 Family Law Reports 574*.

UNITED NATIONS CONVENTION ON THE RIGHTS OF THE CHILD (1989).

WEITHORN, L. and CAMPBELL, S. (1982) 'The competency of children and adults to make informed treatment decisions', *Child Development*, **53**, pp.1589.

# 6    Learning to Listen to Children

*Euan M. Ross*

'Taking seriously what the child has to say' Butler-Sloss (1988).

This chapter is written by a paediatrician who teaches medical students but conveys principles that should be applicable to students of all disciplines who are learning to work for children. It is a not an academic treatise, more a personal distillation of practice points gained from inspired teachers from many disciplines, particularly those who worked with the National Children's Bureau in its early days. There is an emphasis on child protection because this tests our skills the most and has the greatest implications when we fail.

Do 'professional people' — to give a generic title that in this chapter covers the host of social workers, doctors, nurses, lawyers, therapists, teachers, clergy, police, magistrates (putting them in no rank order of significance) — have any inbuilt or preordained ability to communicate with children? I think not. It is only in recent years that the insights of those who have made deep study into the needs of children have trickled into everyday practice.

In the UK there has been a welcome increase in interest in communication with children in the past two decades much fostered by organizations such as the National Children's Bureau, Action for Sick Children, NSPCC, RSPCC and many others. Much has been written about the development of language in children and its pathology and even more about child protection (Law and Conway, 1992). Shield and Baum (1994) stressed the need to listen to children when treatment plans are being formulated, and discussed the chronological age at which children can be expected to make an informed decision about treatment. 'Children who are legally too young to give consent to treatment must still be treated as individuals whose rights as members of society are not solely dependant on the legal definition of the day' (p.1192). They were subsequently censured for their approach in correspondence from North America in subsequent issues of the *British Medical Journal*. Davie (1993), points out the paucity of literature written from the perspective of those who listen to and try to make sense of what they hear.

## 'Have Ye Not Heard, Have Ye Not Understood?'

There is an essential difference between hearing and listening. New born babies can hear perfectly well once their ear canals have dried out. They have to learn to make sense of what they hear; this takes many years, some despite having perfectly formed hearing never fully achieve it. As parents or as professionals working with children we may still have a great deal to learn about the art of listening. No one can fully appreciate classical music without some teaching: we can go on courses to learn how to listen to music and emerge able to get much more out of the great classics than before. The same goes for listening to children.

We need to be taught how to listen to them, it is not an intuitive matter though some find it easier than others. Whilst all professionals have to pass examinations based on expected knowledge, we are not routinely examined in attitudinal and listening skills. To some extent we learn them informally from outstanding teachers but this cannot be guaranteed and some teachers are negative role models in this respect.

### How Can We Learn to Listen?

Firstly we have to be able to listen to adults; this in itself is not always easy. We have all been accused of failing to listen by our nearest and dearest. Those less nearly related may be too polite and fail to correct us when we need it the most. However, the repeated waves of attack on the child care professions should have sensitized us all to the conclusion that matters go seriously wrong when we do not listen to children. This is repeatedly stressed in the Cleveland and subsequent reports into child abuse (Butler-Sloss, 1988).

- All too often we believe nonsense told us by people of any age and all too readily trust those who should not be trusted and fail to appreciate great lies. Example — 'Munchausen by proxy' of which the most topical and tragic example is the case where a nursing auxiliary managed to kill several infants in hospital before being suspected.

- Equally, we fail to listen to the truth when it is being told to us by children — as a result gross injustice has been done — as in the Cleveland, Orkney (Asquith, 1993) and other child abuse cases where children who were ultimately accepted as telling the truth were not understood at the time.

- We speak too much but we rarely listen — a regular failing of politicians — (both professional ones and the grumbling amateurs in the staff tea room).

- Communicating with children is a different matter from being kind to or fond of them, or being very skilled at coping with their physical needs.

Some who cannot communicate successfully with adults seek their audience among children. Many of the best known children's authors come in to this category. Examples include Enid Blyton, Lewis Carroll and J M Barrie. One reads of the childhood unhappiness expressed in the autobiographies of the famous — how much more common this must be in the unpublished annals of the poor. Having empathy and thus the ability to communicate with children is a skill which can be learned. Is it laziness or some inherent defect of character if one persists in a career involving children without becoming aware of one's lack of listening skills and seeking to improve them?

### Telephone Listening

The telephone is not a true substitute for direct contact. One can only fully learn about a child's needs from first-hand knowledge which comes from personal observation and informed listening, seeing and smelling. The telephone can give opportunities for listening that otherwise might be impossible but we need to evaluate the role of the telephone in listening to children in British child care practice. Phone installation has spread to nearly every home in Britain. 'Rich kids' are starting to acquire their own portable telephones. Will the television-phone become the next household 'essential'? In the USA the concept of telephone consultations at set times which can be pre-booked are becoming routine. Will, or should, this practice spread to the UK? In sparsely populated rural areas such as outback Australia life saving advice can be given over the phone even to young children.

Many countries are now setting up forms of telephone Helplines for children along similar lines to the British 'Childline', but there is a great deal to learn about their role and use and abuse, including the consequences if the phone cannot be answered. Fortunately the organizations that run them are putting great effort into training their telephone listeners. Telephone providers make great profits — they know. Yet the advertisement which urges us that 'It's good to talk' ignores the fact that those who need to talk the most are the least likely to have ready access to a phone or the necessary supply of coins. They are unlikely to talk to 'the listening bank'.

### The Sleeping or Unconscious Child

One cannot communicate with a sleeping child. Jasmine Beckford died from abuse and neglect, she and her sibling had been observed at sleep in a darkened room by their social worker who had been assured that they were well. She did not wish to disturb them, thus Jasmine was never seen awake in her final months (Blom-Cooper, 1985).

- If you do not wish to disturb you must make a point of returning until you are satisfied that you have seen the child in an active state, functioning normally.

As a children's doctor one recalls that, whilst there are times when technical excellence is the greatest need, on other occasions lack of communication skills and inability to listen to children are more likely to lead to misdiagnosis than endless investigation. In a West Coast USA hospital a child of 8 had been 'barking like a seal' for several months. She had been through extensive investigations including biopsy of her inflamed vocal cords. Listening to her hoarse voice between the barks soon revealed that she and her troubled mother both had a great need to seek attention. Family therapy, not more biopsies and medicines were the answer.

## Staff Selection and Training

Thirty years ago the concept of child abuse had hardly been recognized, and naturally did not figure in professional training let alone formal teaching in communication skills. It thus can be expected that professional workers aged much over fifty will have had little systematic training in their undergraduate courses on matters specific to child abuse and have had to rely on whatever postgraduate training they have attended. This may have been fragmentary and unplanned.

How do we train ourselves, our students and our seniors to listen to children? The 'right' attitudes are needed at the top in any organization. Senior members need to teach by example (as well as in the classroom) about personal strengths and weaknesses. There are times when they have to take the difficult step of asking the very questions that those more junior to themselves would like to ask but do not dare. They must be seen to be supporting training sessions and stay for the whole course leaving others to go to the 'cannot be missed' committees that steal their days.

## Teaching Aids and Hindrances

In clinical training students are often hidden behind one-way screens in over-warm side rooms to observe developmental assessments and psychiatric interviews. It is important that teachers are properly trained in the use of one-way screens. It is all too easy to forget the student. Such screens should be used sparingly. There are quite enough children with problems for all students to be able to join sessions — but singly, not in groups. Often they can be a useful intermediary as they are likely to be nearer the parent's age than their instructor: They may have more talent for listening than their instructor. Even videotaping the simplest interview with co-operative and informed consenting participants can be most revealing. One can analyze body language as well as speech. Among medical teachers, general practice has paved the way in video teaching and this example is spreading slowly to other disciplines. Well-made video teaching films in small doses are good for demonstrating educational points; they must be made to professional standards and heavily edited. Videos must be watched with a teacher present who can stop the tape when appropriate and start immediate discussion. Otherwise they can readily become a bore.

### How Do We Listen to Children?

Total listening uses all one's senses and includes seeing, smelling, feeling as well as hearing. Usually it is a joy to listen to children but not always. It can be exhausting, often a great deal of time is needed before a child can unburden his / her mind to you. What one is told may worry one greatly; any hint that one is not really interested or needs to be doing something else will destroy the relationship. Should the child be with their parents? Under what circumstances should both parties be seen separately? There is no easy answer. Older children can be very defensive and arrogant in parental company and then suddenly change to sweet reasonableness when on their own. I often ask the child to help me make the tea. The key is not to 'take sides' nor allow oneself to be set up.

Much of one's experience with adults is highly relevant to children — remember the times when you have been angry with professional people, even felt like going to law? Your problem probably had its basis in 'Nobody listened to me' rather than incompetence in knowledge or action, 'I could have told him that.'

Those who speak do not always say what they mean, listeners must be able to hear between the lines. In a medical context, the request, 'Can I have some more of the cough mixture?' — may be followed by a lingering grasp on the door handle — 'While I'm here, doctor . . .'. Then the real problem pours out — the pornographic magazines that her husband brings home, the worries about the child's over-sexualized language or suspicions of illegal drug taking. One is told these tales only if one is ready to hear them. The perils to the child if one is not prepared to listen can be very serious. 'I did not tell the doctor as he is always so busy.' Other professions can quote parallel scenarios.

All that applies to adults applies to children but there is more.

Children develop rapidly. In the normal child, growth and development proceed harmoniously; these two aspects are dissociated in handicapped children. Dr Mary Sheridan's *Children's Developmental Progress* (1973) remains a key text on child development. Knowledge of human development, both normal and abnormal is a prerequisite to learning to communicate with children.

### Is This Child, Doing Things, Hearing and Seeing like Other Children?

If a professional worker, parent, teacher or child has worries on any of these issues, multi-disciplinary developmental assessment is needed. This needs a very wide span of knowledge. A large number of conditions/problems may need to be excluded through structured listening and a few well targeted investigations. Tragedies occur if such problems are not taken seriously.

## The Setting — Permission to Speak

The surroundings must be right. They must be child-friendly with an appearance appropriate to children. One must cater for a wide range of ages and tastes. Let your clinic/office look like a happy child's own room. The listening person must seem right, look right, smell right. Neither the starched collar nor the torn jeans nor an overpowering smell from out of a bottle nor lack of soap and water! All too often professional workers overwhelm children. In an attempt to be friendly they ask the child's name or age, not appreciating that young children are unused to meeting someone who does not know them already. The listener must be credible to the child and those who bring the child along. Even very young children will clam up in the presence of those who do not 'seem right' to them.

Some children are known by a different name from the one written on their records. Children hate being accused of being the wrong age or sex! A few enquiries behind the scenes can get the relationship right from the start. How much privacy is needed? Is a chaperone needed? How many should be in the room? One student is usually enough. People will talk about most intimate matters to empathic strangers, as illustrated by radio phone-ins.

Very minor and inexpensive measures can make a great difference in the appearance of a room. If forensic interviews are to be undertaken, video cameras and remote microphones may be needed; they must be so positioned to be as unthreatening as possible.

## Ways of Listening

Children need time to sum up new situations;

- When they arrive semi-ignore them, set out your room with appropriate books, crayons, paper.

- Do not provide toys/playthings for the wrong age. Children can be easily insulted. If you get this wrong the child may rightly regard you as untrustworthy.

This particularly applies to the use of dolls with genitalia. The use of anatomically correct dolls should be left to those trained in this field. Although many such dolls have been produced in recent years there is much difference of opinion concerning their validity; just because a child finds them interesting and may try some suggestive experiments does not prove that they have been abused or are grossly precocious. They should not be used routinely and then only by those with full training in their use.

## Speaking Through Drawing (Thomas and Silk, 1990)

One of the great differences in child and adult behaviour is the desire to draw. Few adults draw much, children do it every day. Even if your attempts at verbal communication are failing, paper and pencil offer the best alternative. If you speak a different language from the child you can still communicate through drawings. Sometimes children will only express their emotions through a drawing. Do not ask children to draw something complicated. Ask them to draw a picture of where they live and see what happens. When looking at the drawing do not over-interpret it. Has a happy or sad picture been drawn? What size are the members of the family? Is one much larger than the others? What are they doing? Have genitalia been drawn? How many parents were drawn. (I saw a picture that included 'big dad' and 'little dad'.) A six year old boy brought because of 'behaviour problems' told me that he would like to draw a picture of the ghost that lived in his house and that 'the ghost had no kidneys'. The ghost turned out to be an elder sibling born without kidneys who died when twenty-four hours old. This child was the replacement.

Examinations can be speeded up if parents are routinely asked to bring up some recent school books. The marks and teachers comments can be most revealing too.

## Who Should Do the Listening?

Those with ears to hear. Those who cannot listen to adults can be assumed to be incapable of listening to children. Some people of high academic ability are very poor listeners — they may be 'too full of themselves'. Some get hung up on untenable theories — one year it is exclusion diets, then anal dilatation, the next is false memory syndrome. Be boringly adverse to fashions — 'Be not the first by whom the new is tried' if you wish to protect children. But not the last by whom the old is set aside.

We must not subject people — children or adults — to repeated examination. Detective work is for trained detectives, not the rest of us. Stories change, either time heals or magnifies, often a bit of both so that the truth may remain hazy.

## Special Attention Needs to be Paid To:

- Listening even before the child is born. Just as the obstetrician and midwife listen with a fetal stethoscope and its much more sophisticated electronic successors one must listen to the words that the pregnant mother says — or does not say about her pregnancy because they foretell a great deal about her attitude to her unborn child. Beware the pregnant mother who appears to be hostile to her pregnancy or the mother who has made no physical preparation for her new baby. (Winnicott, 1988 and frequently elsewhere in his other classic writings in this field.)

- In the early days of life one can identify at least five different types of cry — pain, hunger, boredom, illness and the cerebral cry of the brain injured baby. The child's development of feeding and smiling and the baby's expression of both contentment and anger are revealing. (Wolff, 1969)

- Learn to recognize the older abused child who develops frozen watchfulness, who cringes readily, as well as the one who 'settles in easily' — who is over-friendly to any stranger who shows the slightest interest.

Children speak with meaning at very varying ages. All parents know to be careful what they say in front of children, and know the embarrassments that can occur. Students need to learn a great deal about normal and abnormal child development. It is essential that they appreciate how great are the variations among normal children. This particularly applies to the rate of development of speech. Some have a much earlier ability not only to speak but to communicate effectively.

### Is the Child Telling the Truth?

Young children speak the truth as they understand it. Peter Ustinov recalled how following Sunday School teaching he refused to visit Father Christmas at Harrods in London, believing it to be an establishment run by King Herod. It is too easy to be wrong — all of us tend to say the thing that we feel is wanted of us. We all know that children's understanding of trust is a developing matter. Children are blessed with insight and imagination that tends to be lost or knocked out of us as we age. Children may be very protective towards an abusive parent and may have been threatened with dire consequences if they tell the truth — remember Oliver Twist.

### Can't Speak the Language?

A Russian boy on holiday in the UK was brought to see me in (parental) hope that I would repeat his prescription for drugs for attention deficit disorder. Neither of us could speak the same language but that hardly mattered. We started with noughts and crosses, then a quick game of snakes and ladders before a walk down the road where he read out makes of car, including turbos and fuel injection models. He was a bright lad cooped up at home in a small flat. He probably had underachieving school mates. Nothing wrong with his attention.

One can over-readily assume that people from ethnic minority backgrounds in the UK do not know any English, but even many immigrants can speak enough to communicate if they are put at ease. Interpreters cannot be guaranteed to give a true translation and may give a 'sanitised' version. Do not fall into the trap of believing that only people of the same race and culture understand each other. Beware caste differences or inter-racial disputes, political correctness or collusion. Some men find the concept of senior professional women workers, especially social workers, very difficult to relate to yet demand that 'their' women folk are only seen by women. The difficulty is to reach these women and their children.

One trap is to be deceived because a patient/client happens to be part of one's extended family, church, golf club or a private patient of a colleague. Where personal loyalties are involved, one must step aside and make sure that a totally non-involved colleague takes over. Some parents have the skills to make life very difficult for those who are trying to give professional help to children. I recall great problems where the father was a barrister, the mother a solicitor, and their child was showing signs of abuse.

## Dialect

With increasing mobility of professional people the child's dialect and yours may be quite different. Words describing child behaviour let alone their genitalia can be totally different even within a country. How many words for penis can be recorded in the UK? How many English know the Scots expression for unemployment benefit, 'the buroo' (pronounced brew) or the subtle difference between 'girning' and 'greetin'? Some words may be so naughty in the family context that they cannot be spoken. Few non-medical people whatever their age and education know where their major internal organs are or what they do. Doctors learn at least 10,000 new words during their training. They emerge with very different concepts — say of the stomach or the bowels — from that of society as a whole and forget that they can easily be talking at cross purposes even with other professionals.

## Making Time . . . Make Time (Miss Piggy to Kermit — on Numerous Occasions)

It takes time to make a trusting relationship with a child and family. Whilst most professional people are genuinely and sometimes grossly overworked and have to limit the time they spend on any one case, it can be too easy to plead lack of time and take short cuts. The answer usually lies in better management of the limited time that one has. Advice and training in managing one's time may be needed. Time is easily dissipated in writing over-long reports or attending too many meetings. Some, without realizing it, actually enjoy the role of worker-martyr. Some have treatable health problems that limit efficiency. It is all too easy to become insidiously unfit and marginally yet chronically depressed and become over-cautious. Some with these problems were badly taught or are poorly supervized.

### Taking the History

The first and cardinal skill taught to clinical medical students applies also to all other professions — namely history taking — structured and active listening not physical examination or biochemical tests. Other disciplines have their own or the equivalent devices or procedures. History taking in itself can be powerfully therapeutic and is one of the core skills of all professions — but is not mastered by all. There are certain aspects to this craft which are often overlooked:

- With older children address the questions directly to them, let them answer in their own words and watch whether their parents feed them answers or put them in to their minds.

- Ask structured questions in a set order so that one does not leave out relevant areas:

- Make accurate and legible records: always write in précis the gist of what the patient actually said: if they say 'I have pain doing number two's, do not write 'bowels'! If the child actually says 'migraine' they may have heard an adult with a headache using the word and there can be no guarantee that the child actually has this problem.

- Beware the leading question. All too often the amateur asks a question that suggests only one answer: a child has a large mark probably caused by a whip over the back — 'What did daddy hit you with?' That is a typical leading question. Try again: 'I see you have a red mark on your back. Can you tell me how it happened?' Record the answers you get. If you ask leading questions you are very likely to get the answer that the interviewee thinks you want!

The standard way that medical students are taught to take history could with profit be applied to other professions concerned with child care. The universal first question is: 'Why have you come to see me?' — then the *History of the main presenting problem* followed by the: *Previous (medical) history* then the:

*Family History*

- Including the health of the mother, father, siblings. It is important that you as well as the patient decide what is relevant and that all deaths and possibly inherited disorders in the family are disclosed.

*Social History*

- The housing, where the family live, their moves, how far from relatives, who is in work and what do they do, are there major social problems? Transport, amenities, even sometimes the name and breed of the dog! There is a fine line between being gratuitously nosy and getting vital and relevant information.

Some additional information is particularly relevant in medicine but should also be relevant to any professional worker:

*Childbirth and Development*

- The mother's health in pregnancy — did she have a straight forward or difficult pregnancy and delivery? A bad experience can colour her attitude to the child for better or worse.

- Where was the child born, birth weight, health as a new baby, feeding and behaviour patterns?

- The ages at which the child did things such as walking, talking, nursery and school experience and grades.

It is only when this stage is concluded that doctors should want to start a medical examination: With any luck by now the child will be playing or drawing. Note if they separate from a parent or not, whether their behaviour is age-appropriate. Do child and parent interact, talk to each other, reassure each other, cling or seem indifferent? Does the parent speak ill of the child in their hearing? Does the child speak ill of the parent?

## A Note for Medical Readers

It has now become exceptional for a child to be smelly or dressed in worn clothes — does the child over-readily part with clothes, or refuse? Some children are most hesitant to let their genital regions be inspected, others immediately masturbate. Watch for spontaneous over-sexualized speech. I find the time well spent watching this process out of the corner of my eye and do not want pre-stripped children brought to me. This often tells me more than actual physical inspection of the genitalia and anus where, unless there has been very recent trauma or repeated buggery, there are generally no convincing physical signs to confirm or deny that penetrative sexual abuse has occurred.

In the course of listening to a child or in the course of physical examination it may dawn on you that the child may have been sexually abused — what then? You are now confronted with an ethical dilemma. You know that repeated physical examination is contraindicated; if you have not had forensic training your findings are likely to be wide open to challenge. You also know that only a fresh collection of secretions for bacteriology and detection of spermatozoa will be of any forensic value and that ano-genital tears heal rapidly. Unless you are appropriately trained the correct course is to complete your examination in the conventional way inspecting the ano-genital regions as you would in any other paediatric examination, making careful records of what you see at the same time. You should remember to look at the skin, fundi, eardrums and upper lip fraenum, making careful, dated and signed notes as you go.

You should ensure an immediate forensic examination by those appointed to undertake one in line with the Child Protection procedures of your area.

## Teaching Staff to Listen to Children

Some are likely to have had much more recent training than others. In-house teaching is far more cost-effective than sending people away on courses, because the skills gained are shared in the department. When people do go on courses at the expense of your budget, insist that they write up notes and then give a presentation to the department so that everyone gains. Identify those in the department who are poor listeners and communicators and institute remedial help, for those who cannot be taught — shoo them sideways and away from children.

If you are a manager, particularly if recently appointed, you will have inherited most of your staff and it is usually a long time before you will have recruited your 'own' team. It is necessary to evaluate their listening to children skills, you may find it difficult to get a chance to see them in action under real life situations. When interviewing your staff, make a list of the training in the subject that they have actually had. In a successful commercial business it is a general rule that about 5 per cent of professional staff time needs to be spent on in-service training. The same is true for work with children. Remember that some become less skilled with the passage of time, and none can be expert in every aspect of their work.

## Conclusion

Listening to children is not a vague concept or something that is purely a natural gift or even readily picked up. Listening and understanding what you hear requires a trained and practised ear. The quality of listening among those who work for children is greatly influenced by those who lead departments. If leaders have these skills, appreciate how they gained them from valued colleagues in a wide variety of disciplines and are prepared to value and teach them to their colleagues, the quality of professional work for children will rise and the risks of failure to protect them will diminish

## References

ARGYLE, M. (1988) *Bodily Communication*, (2nd ed) London, Routledge.

ASQUITH, S. (Ed) (1993) *Protecting Children Cleveland to Orkney: More Lessons to Learn?*, London, HMSO.

BLOM-COOPER, L. (1985) *A Child in Trust: The Report of the Panel of Inquiry Into the Circumstances Surrounding the Death of Jasmine Beckford*, London, HMSO.

BUTLER-SLOSS, E. (1988) *Report of the Inquiry into Child Abuse in Cleveland 1987*, London, HMSO.

DAVIE, R. (1993) 'Listen to the child: A time for change', *The Psychologist*, June, pp.252–57.

LAW, J. and CONWAY, J. (1992) *Child Abuse and Neglect: The Effect on Communication Development. A Review of the Literature*, London, AFASIC.

LOCKE, J.L. (1995) *The Child's Path to Spoken Language*, Cambridge, Harvard University Press.

SHERIDAN, M. (1973) *Children's Development from Birth to Five*, Slough, NFER.

SHIELD, J.P.H. and BAUM, J.D. (1994) 'Children's consent to treatment: Listen to the children — they will have to live with the decision', *British Medical Journal*, **308**, pp.1192–1193.

THOMAS, G.V. and SILK, A.M.J. (1990) *An Introduction to the Psychology of Children's Drawing*, New York, Harvester Wheatsheaf.

WINNICOTT, D. (1988) 'Communication between infant and mother and mother and infant compared and contrasted', *Babies and Their Mothers*, Free Association Books.

WOLFF, P.H. (1969) 'The natural history of crying and other vocalisations in early infancy', in FOSS, B.M. (Ed) *Determinants of Infant Behaviour*, London, Methuen.

*Part II*

*Generic Issues*

# 7 Listening to Children with Disabilities and Special Educational Needs

*Philippa Russell*

## Introduction

My disability is a fundamental factor in the person that is 'me'. I do not want to deny this by calling myself 'a person with special needs' nor any other euphemism, nor do I want to deny the collective identity we (disabled people) have achieved for ourselves. Therefore I am a disabled person and proud of it. (Micheline Mason, 1992)

We (disabled people) reject the inhumanity of the 'medical model' of thinking involved in labelling and identifying people by their impairing conditions. Calling someone a 'Down's child' or a 'spina bif' makes the child no more than their condition . . . the social model of disability identifies prejudice and discrimination in institutions, policies, structures and the whole environment of our society as the principle for our exclusion . . . we must reject the legacy of the past that has excluded us and see children as they really are — not 'categories' but as citizens and with contributions to make, if we let them. (Micheline Mason, 1994)

The past decade has seen major advances in the creation of working partnerships between parents and schools (and a range of other services) working with children with disabilities and special educational needs. The concept of 'partnership with parents', promulgated in the Warnock Committee, is reiterated in the Children Act 1989 and in the Education Act 1993 and the Code of Practice. The shift to partnership and 'empowerment' of parents has reflected a growing recognition that firstly professional services can seldom be wholly effective without parental support and secondly has demonstrated that 'partnership' (however defined) is not an easy option. Many families have external factors in their own lives which make partnership problematic. Families and children do not necessarily agree and some children present problems in the family as well as in the school context.

But partnership with parents has also clearly demonstrated that children are also key factors in any assessment or planning arrangements. The Children Act 1989 broke new ground in emphasizing the 'paramount importance' of the welfare of the child in any planning arrangements or decision making process. The UK ratification of the UN Convention on the Rights of the Child further underwrote the mutual responsibilities of professionals and parents to take account of children's views and to facilitate those views being heard. The introduction to the Code of Practice therefore states (for the first time in education guidance) that:

> Special educational provision will be most effective when those responsible take into account the ascertainable wishes of the child concerned, considered in the light of his or her age and understanding. (DFE, 1994, Section 1.3, p.3))

Like the Children Act 1989, the Code of Practice acknowledges that positive partnership with pupils with disabilities or special educational needs is unlikely to occur spontaneously. Careful attention, guidance and encouragement will be required to help pupils respond relevantly and fully. Many young people with special needs may be unaware of the significance of their disability or difficulty and currently few are given direct responsibility for their own progress. But the new school-based and statutory assessment arrangements will require some radical re-thinking by schools, families and any relevant professionals about what pupils think and feel about assessment and any subsequent interventions or support services.

   The genuine involvement of children with disabilities or special educational needs in assessment will be challenging for all concerned. Notwithstanding the key principle of involvement of children in decision-making across the Children Act 1989 and throughout guidance and regulations, the Children Act Report 1993 (presented to Parliament as required under Section 83(6) of the Children Act 1989) noted:

> It was not the general habit of the staff (in four authorities inspected by the Social Services Inspectorate) to ask disabled children how they felt about decisions affecting their daily life or their futures and their views were not routinely recorded on case files. There was also a wide disparity in the levels of skill and expertise of staff working with disabled children, which gave rise to concern. (SSI, 1994, 5.3.2, p.23)

The Children Act Report's conclusions about the training needs of staff providing social care for children with disabilities or special needs can be mirrored in education services. Over the past few years, there have been important initiatives in working directly with pupils with a range of disabilities and special educational needs (for example the work of Irvine Gersch in Waltham Forest — see Chapter 2), but the concept and the context of pupil participation remain challenging. Gersch concluded that all schools needed to consider how to:

   1   Involve pupils in decision-making processes;

2   Determine the pupil's level of participation, taking into account approaches to assessment and intervention which are suitable for his or her age, ability and past experiences.

3   Record pupils' views in identifying their difficulties, setting goals, agreeing a development strategy; monitoring and reviewing progress;

4   Involve pupils in implementing individual education plans.

Gersch's analysis of the key tasks for schools to work upon in order to achieve real participation mirror a report by the Social Services Inspectorate of the first national inspection of services for children with disabilities in England and Wales (SSI, 1994). The Children Act 1989 was a landmark for children with disabilities and their families because for the first time it included services for this 'category' of children and families within a mainstream framework of services for all children. The shift from a 'medical' model of disability to a 'social model' of disability had been as challenging for many social services departments as increased integration of children with often complex needs within mainstream education had been for their education counterparts. The Children Act 1989 places new duties on social services departments to actively involve children in planning their own futures, *including* children with disabilities and special needs. Volume 6 of the Children Act guidance (*Children with Disabilities*, 1992) acknowledges the challenge, stating that:

> There is a fine balance between giving the child [with a disability or special need] a voice and encouraging them to make informed decisions — and over-burdening them with decision-making procedures where they have insufficient experience and knowledge to make appropriate judgments without additional support. (Section 6.6, p.14)

Although relatively few schools have probably experienced direct conflicts of interest as expressed by children and parents, the Children Act has given some warning messages about the implications of really listening to children and hearing what they say. The Social Services Inspectorate Report (1994) looked specifically at the process of listening to children with disabilities or special needs and about the process which would be required to be effective. Key messages (of equal relevance to schools and LEAs) included:

1   The need to acknowledge that different parts of the same service will have varying skills and experience in working directly with children.

2   Listening to children can create uncomfortable decisions and test loyalty when an agency has seen itself working primarily with *parents*.

3   Linguistic, social, cultural and religious factors will all influence what children say and how they express their views.

4  Participation skills can be learned and children who are regularly involved in decision-making at all levels will be more confident and
competent when major decisions are required.

5  Access to independent advocacy, representation and befriending may be
crucial (particularly when a child is 'looked after' by the local authority). But advocacy will be a sensitive issue for parents and many families
will themselves need support when difficult decisions have to be made.

6  Some children with disabilities and special needs have major communication problems. Access to independent interpreters will be critical —
but it should not be assumed that they have nothing to say!

The SSI, like the Audit Commission (1994) has also stressed the importance of
education and social services departments working together more effectively,
but achieving integrated assessment arrangements which involve parents *and*
children will not be easy. Gersch (1994) has commented that some young
people will need considerable support but emphasizes that the purpose of involving pupils with special needs in assessment and decision-making has the aim
of 'encouraging the young person's *active* involvement in the assessment process.
The (adult) helper will need to know the young person well, to remain impar-
tial and yet to know when to prompt and encourage without implanting their
own ideas.' Gersch (see Chapter 2) describes the importance of 'tracking children' and of needing to 'get inside children's shoes'. He also acknowledges, like
SSI, the challenge of multiple assessment processes and the dangers of losing
children's views and experiences in complex processes.

But the work of SSI and of LEAs like Waltham Forest indicates that there
is a new interest across education and social services to listen to and involve
children with disabilities and special needs. It is therefore helpful to look at the
limited literature and to learn from the direct experiences of children and adults
who have grown up with a disability or special need and who feel able to share
their experiences about how they found 'a voice'.


### Finding a Voice

When I had English exams at school, I would have nightmares and
sleep-walk the night before. I always had the same nightmare, and it
stopped when I left school. It was cushions, big cushions and everything in the room looked far away . . . I tried to study in this dream,
the nightmare. I could feel myself going into it, the nightmare, and it
was always before an exam . . . I used to look for a window to get out.
My aunty saved me once from literally jumping out of the bedroom
window. She just managed to grab me before I jumped out. (Mellor,
1983)

**Miss Can't** is someone who can't do things. She can't walk easily and needs crutches. She gets puffed out and eats too many sweets. She lives with her parents and her mum looks after her. She stays at home all the time unless she gets her brother to take her out. She was behind at school and the teacher took no notice of her 'cos she had learning difficulties. She had to go on a bus, a disabled bus. She's slow at writing and she's stupid at maths. She doesn't know how to use money. She can't find her way around and she has a miserable life. She wishes she was slim; clever; working; could have parties and she would like to learn to go around London. (Imaginary woman described by a young women's group, Russell and Wertheimer (in press))

I guess if you go about feeling like a mouldy artichoke, people tend to react to you as though you were one! I was so shy, especially with boys, that very few managed to overcome their reactions to my disability and my self consciousness enough for any conversation to last more than five minutes, thus affirming my belief that I was unlovable. However, one or two confident souls broke through to me despite all this . . . at some point during those two years I worked out that the cosy future my family had planned for me would be so boring that I would rather die than make their gloomy prophecies come true. When the chance came for me to go to a boarding school for girls with disabilities I jumped at it. I saw it as the beginning of my real road to freedom . . . there were other young people who had gone through all that doubting too. Nice people! Other young women who had their self image as women so severely damaged that they wondered also if they were entitled to anything life had to offer. My three years with nearly one hundred young women with disabilities began a slow healing process. We laughed and cried together. We experienced illness and even deaths amongst us. But we felt so strong! There I discovered what sharing meant and accepting people's differences whether they be of colour, class, religion or experience of disability. I began to accept my differences, my uniqueness, as something to be proud of. (Micheline Mason, 1992)

The three accounts of the challenges (and in Micheline's case) of the triumphs of living with a disability or special educational need remind us all of the need to understand the often mixed emotions (and consequent mixed messages) we may perceive in children and young people with disabilities or special needs. Doug Mellor, quoted above, developed a coping strategy of pretence. He 'learned' by heart the relevant pages of his reading books and he avoided if possible any confrontation with the pain of being illiterate and having learning difficulties. In adult life he was to edit a book setting out a wide range of experiences of growing up with a learning difficulty.

The young women's group, with their imaginary figure of 'Miss Can't' were learning to discuss the sensitive and painful issue of their own disabilities and learning difficulties and their low self esteem. None of the young women had ever had any peer discussions about their special needs; they saw themselves as less capable, less attractive and more hopeless than any external observer would have believed them to be. But the group solidarity enabled them to talk openly to their teachers (and more problematically to their parents) about how they saw the future; what their own educational priorities were during their final years at school and how their poor social skills could be enhanced and developed.

Micheline Mason, the third commentator, is now Chairperson of the Integration Alliance, a leading disability equality trainer and the parent of a disabled daughter. She vividly describes her own process of empowerment — and like the 'Miss Can't' Group she reminds us of the importance of solidarity and sharing experiences. The experience of disability or special needs can be a lonely one. Many teachers (like GPs and social workers) will meet very few children with disabilities in a professional lifetime. Disability equality issues are seldom as integral a component in school policy as are race and gender issues. Children may be seen as more disabled than they are — or they may be perceived as more capable, with less support consequently offered.

## Unequal Opportunities? — Growing Up Disabled

Fish (1986), in a study for the OECD on transition to adult life, highlighted four key aims for education for all young people, namely:

1 The development of a sense of personal identity, personal autonomy and self advocacy

2 The ultimate aim of employment, useful work or a valued activity

3 Social participation, community involvement, leisure and recreational activities

4 The achievement of new roles and responsibilities within and beyond the family.

Fish hypothesized that all young people go through many transitions, but children and young people with disabilities often face additional obstacles in achieving these four key objectives. A number of national studies supported his concerns, in particular Thomas (1989), Brimblecombe and Tripp (1985) and Hirst, Parker and Cozens (1991) who all identified particular problems for many young people and the need for much greater awareness by health, education and social services of the importance of supporting and listening to children with disabilities at a much earlier stage and not only as they moved into adult life.

Because of growing concern about the life experiences of children and young people with disabilities and special needs, Hirst and Baldwin (1994) carried out the first national survey which interviewed children and young people with and without disabilities about their life experiences, their expectations and about the extent to which they felt in control of their own futures. The survey conclusions offer important lessons for schools and LEAs seeking to implement the principles of the Code of Practice — and for social services departments in the context of Children Act and community care policies.

Hirst and Baldwin firstly concluded that having a disability or special need does *not* always mean feeling disempowered and rejected. Many young people interviewed felt as confident and good about themselves as any other young people in the community. But young people with disabilities were in general more likely to report feelings which reflected lack of personal worth, responsibility and self-determination. Self-confidence in general deteriorated rapidly with the severity of the disability, but Hirst and Baldwin found some evidence that even very severely disabled young people felt much more positive if they had more control over their everyday lives and if they were assisted to be more independent. Negative experiences increased with severity of disability but many young people with very minor problems also experienced negative self esteem and had low expectations. Expectations were however positively affected by the attitudes of the pupil's school and also by his or her access to good quality leisure activities — an important reminder of the need to see children holistically and to acknowledge that many young people with disabilities have very circumscribed lives.

The Hirst and Baldwin study has implications for schools and LEAs. Section 3.8 of the Code of Practice reminds schools that when they refer children to the LEA for statutory assessment, they should submit information on 'the recorded views of parents and, where appropriate, children on the earlier stages of assessment and any action and support to date'. The new requirement to provide written individual education plans at stages two and three of school-based assessment should provide a framework for such recording and for positive action. Assessment can be very threatening for parents. It may appear even more threatening for a pupil, particularly where he or she fears exclusion from a school or is experiencing a loss of self-esteem because of poor performance as compared to friends.

Statutory assessment may similarly pose problems, particularly if the pupil concerned is uncertain as to how he or she may express views or how those views will be considered if they are perhaps critical of a particular aspect of school life or of family or other professionals within the child's local community. However, Hirst and Baldwin offer clear messages about the importance of giving young people with a disability a sense of control over their own lives and the need to enable young people to 'practise' decision-making right from the start (and not only when a significant decision has to be made).

### Listening to Children with Disabilities: Understanding Disability and Special Health Care Needs

Hirst and Baldwin (1994) remind us that the children and young people in their comparative study were significantly more likely to report that they had a health problem if they were disabled. Therefore child health services, which usually have long-term knowledge of a particular child and the impact of a health problem or disability upon educational progress, have a critical role in assessment — sometimes as an advocate as well as a source of direct information on the health issue in question. Children may be more concerned by the day-to-day impact of a disability or medical problem than by its longer term consequences. The management of incontinence problems or personal care in a busy and large secondary school may have disproportionate negative effects upon the achievements of a child with a moderate disability. Brimblecombe and Tripp (1985) and Hirst and Baldwin (1994) both found considerable evidence that young people with disabilities had very limited individual contact with medical advisers. Usually accompanied by parents, many hesitated to raise sensitive issues and there were often significant misunderstandings about the purpose of treatment; the management of incontinence or medication and about the adult implications (and hence career opportunities) of the particular medical condition or disability. Health services, like their education and social services counterparts, may be challenged in involving children and young people in decision-making.

The Children Act 1989 confirmed that children — subject to sufficient maturity — can legally refuse examinations or treatment, but recent work by Alderson (1994) and Bax (1990) and others has demonstrated that children **can** be involved in very traumatic medical decision-making processes and that honest discussions about disability or medical conditions are often much less frightening than the imagined future based on half-understood information or negative media images of conditions like cancer.

The Department of Health's draft guidance, *Child Health in the Community: a Guide to Good Practice* (1995), reiterates the central principle of the Court Report that all children should have access to a

> child and family centred service in which skilled help is readily available and accessible; which is integrated in as much as it sees the child as a whole and as a continuously developing person. The DOH guidance, like the Court Report which preceded it, recognises that the biggest challenge to child health (and other statutory services) are the children and families who require long-term care and support. (Section 3.1, p.10)

Schools and education services will need to be sensitive to the implications of any special health care needs at different 'ages and stages'. Many young people — whilst theoretically able to take responsibility for their own medication — fail to take drugs for diabetes, asthma or epilepsy because they wish to deny any degree of dependency and because they are reluctant to appear different within their peer group. Whether the treatment is simply access to an asthma inhaler or arrangements for the administration of rectal valium in the case of epilepsy, children and young people have information to share about when, where and how they would like any treatment to be given. 'Sonia' (Russell and Wertheimer, in press) described her embarrassment at her new mainstream school's handling of her incontinence problem:

> I'm not really incontinent at all now I have an indwelling catheter. All I need is a proper accessible and private loo — with some hot water and soap for my hands afterwards! But it seemed as if I was such a problem, no real understanding of the need for privacy — it was no-one's business but my own. They were frightened of me — til my mum got the adviser from my hospital to talk to them, sort of calm them down. They were actually calling my mum in to help me, as if I was a health and safety risk! Trouble is, they didn't understand my disability [spina bifida]. I wish my special school could have talked to them first. The continence management was better at one school, the curriculum at the other! It's silly isn't it, really they should have talked to me about what I needed and they were too embarrassed to do so. You could say, my catheter had become a special educational need.

Sonia's story is a salutary reminder of involving young people in planning as well as assessment and the need to look holistically at the school environment to ensure it is accessible and user-friendly. Sonia was a confident and competent young woman with a strong sense of humour. But apart from the tussle with incontinence she was also acutely aware of the vulnerability of many young people with disabilities to bullying and teasing without 'whole school policies' to provide appropriate support and intervention. A Sheffield study, (Nabuzoka, 1993), found that children and young people with special needs were three times more likely to experience bullying; name-calling and teasing at school. But the same study found that schools *could* adopt positive strategies; assertiveness training and anti-bullying policies which altered the school environment.

### Supporting Children and Young People with Disabilities and Special Needs

Some schools (and professionals) will find the 'giving of advice and guidance' very challenging, particularly where the pupil concerned is causing problems because of difficult behaviour and where there is uncertainty about both the origins and the management of that behaviour in a school context. However, there are some practical models of support and intervention which can be developed to meet local need. The SSI Inspection of Services for children with disabilities (1994) noted that in some authorities, the use of individual representatives or advocates was helpful when a child or young person needed to be involved in sensitive discussion and decision-making.

The Audit Commission (1994) visited one authority where education and social services had jointly appointed an education liaison officer whose role was to work directly with pupils with problems or special educational needs and to tackle difficulties effectively. A number of social services departments have similarly appointed children's rights officers to provide an independent voice for children and young people when they are 'looked after' by the local authority. Few children's rights officers have currently been closely involved in work with schools, but there is growing recognition that when a child has a special educational need or disability, such involvement may be key in enabling the child to make progress and in planning for a successful future.

Lewis (1993), looking at the attitudes of (and support from) peer groups of pupils in mainstream schools has also highlighted the value of using 'buddies'; peer tutoring; co-operative learning and collaborative learning. She found certain key themes in a wide range of studies which are of considerable importance in creating a positive climate of opinion towards integration for children with severe learning difficulties or with other disabilities in a school setting, namely that other children are part of the solution (as well as the problem) of any difficulties experienced by a pupil with a disability or special need in their peer group. Parent support groups are well established for parents of children with particular disabilities, but there has been limited development in accessing children and young people to a peer group and in ensuring that they meet other young people with similar needs.

### In Conclusion: Thinking about Disability; 'Our Journey of Discovery'

For the past three years, I have been supporting Claire who has severe impairments, — both physical and intellectual — at her local community school. My experiences during this time have been both exciting and painful. Exciting because it has been a journey of discovery for us both.

The journey of discovery has not been without some pain. I had to come to terms with Claire's impairment. In the early days I worked very hard on individual programmes with Claire in the hope that one day she might be able to hold a cup, learn to feed herself or indicate physically what her needs were. I soon realised that this approach . . . did not bring encouraging results. I began to feel incapable, worthless and a failure. I knew I had to find another way so I stopped trying to teach with a capital 'T' and started to listen. Our roles were reversed. Claire had become the teacher and I became the one who was to learn. She certainly does have her own way of communicating; all she needed was someone to listen to her. I stood back and watched the relationships develop with her friends in the classroom. They saw beyond her disability. Communication seems quite natural to them. They had become confident in providing for Claire's additional needs and include her in all their activities as a matter of course. (Carol Sampson, Claire's Personal Assistant, quoted in Mason and Rieser, 1994)

Carol Sampson presents a new and positive image of disability. Her 'help' for Claire has been a learning experience. She sees Claire as a person with wishes and choices and she learns from her about the sort of life she, Claire, wants to have. Listening to children with disabilities or special needs will be a major challenge. Micheline Mason (*op cit*) writing about self-image, impairment and disability in children, comments on some of the challenges. She notes that the well meaning attitude of 'they are all the same as me' is unhelpful. Disabled people often have to invest a lot more effort into doing the same things as their peers. They may have to cope with physical pain, tiredness, discomfort or frustration. Some disabilities or special needs like asthma or epilepsy are intermittent. Life may seem 'normal' and then a sudden recurrence causes changes of plan, disappointment and uncertainty about the future.

Mason (1994) observes that:

> . . . Apart from the effects of the impairment itself, we are also dealing with a relentless oppression which, even if apparently absent from close personal day-to-day relationships, will launch itself at us from bill-boards, television, strangers on the street, officialdom and everywhere else. The fact that we are NOT valued equally is implicit in the whole fabric of society and our culture . . . the struggle to feel good about ourselves as people who are different, is difficult to cope with alone. Racism is now challenged in many schools. But this general awareness has not even begun in most schools for disability. If schools are to support young disabled people who have already internalised much negative conditioning, then the connection with disabled adults need to be made not just as role models but as *real* people leading real lives.

Listening to children and young people with special educational needs or disabilities will present constant challenges. But it is also an opportunity for 'open learning' and a reminder that simplistic expectations about low participation rates and the inability to discuss sensitive issues in a positive way are often confounded. The Code of Practice confirms and amplifies the key messages of the Children Act 1989, namely the right of children to be heard; the positive consequences of pupil involvement in addressing special educational needs and the possibility of developing new partnerships with pupils to complement parent partnership and to ensure that the new approaches to meeting special educational needs as set out in the Code of Practice are understood, implemented and reinforced by all concerned.

As Wade and Moore (1993) comment, in their study of the views of young people with special educational needs and disabilities about experiencing special education, 'for students with disabilities, assessment will always be a two-edged word, referring both to academic performance and to physical progress or deterioration'. But Wade and Moore found many positive messages for listening to and learning from pupils with disabilities. The young people interviewed valued positive feedback on their progress; the organization of classrooms so that learning (and positive peer relationships) were encouraged; opportunities to share leisure and social activities and to take positions of responsibility within the wider school activities. Wade and Moore concluded that individual children's needs could only be met within whole-school policies which were based on explicit values and principles and which included pupils with disabilities and special needs as valued members of the whole school community. The new requirement on all maintained schools to have school policies on special educational needs in place by summer 1995 was an important opportunity to consider **how** pupils' views and needs could be integrated within the school's planning and review arrangements.

Asking the pupils for help may not be easy. Jackie (Russell and Wertheimer, in press) notes that

> We (pupils with special needs) want to let people know what we can do with our mouths, our hands, our brains. We want you to think about what we are saying, what we feel about things. It isn't easy. Don't turn your back on us and try to understand that lots of people on the street have difficulty and writing. Sometimes they treat us like zombies, like people from another planet. But we can speak for ourselves. We would like to do better. Treat us like human beings and we can all work together.

Working together with pupils and children will be the next challenge for the coming decade. It is a challenge — and an opportunity, if we tackle it optimistically.

### References

ALDERSON, P. (1994) *Children's Decisions in Health Care and Research*, London, Institute of Education Social Science Research Unit, London University.

AUDIT COMMISSION (1994) *Seen But Not Heard: Co-ordinating Community Child Health and Social Services for Children in 'Need'*, London, Audit Commission/HMSO.

BAX, M. (1990) 'Young disabled adults: Their needs', *Children and Society*, 4, pp.64–9.

BRIMBLECOMBE, F. and TRIPP, J. (1985) *The Needs of Handicapped Young Adults*, Department of Child Health, University of Exeter.

DFE (1994) *The Code of Practice on the Identification and Assessment of Special Educational Needs*, London, Department for Education.

DEPARTMENT OF HEALTH (1992) *The Children Act Guidance and Regulations, Volume 6, Children with Disabilities*, London, HMSO.

DEPARTMENT OF HEALTH (1994) *Children Act Report 1993*, London, HMSO.

DEPARTMENT OF HEALTH (1995) *Child Health in the Community: A Guide to Good Practice*, London, Department of Health.

GERSCH, I. (1994) *Working Together for Children and Young People: The Student Report*, London Borough of Waltham Forest, Department of Educational Psychology.

GERSCH, I. (1987) 'Involving pupils in their own assessment', in BOWERS, T. (Ed) *Special Educational Needs and Human Resource Management*, London, Croom Helm.

FISH, J. (1986) *Young People with Handicaps: The Road to Adulthood*, Paris, Centre for Educational Research and Innovation, OECD.

HIRST, M. and BALDWIN, S. (1994) *Unequal Opportunities: Growing up Disabled*, York, Social Policy Research Unit, University of York.

HIRST, M., PARKER, G. and COZENS, A. (1991) 'Disabled young people', in OLIVER, M. (Ed) *Social Work: Disabled People and Disabling Environments*, London, Jessica Kingsley.

LEWIS, A. (1993) 'Entitled to learn together?', in ASHDOWN, R., CARPENTER, B. and BOVAIR, K. (Eds) *The Curriculum Challenge*, London, Falmer Press.

MASON, M. (1981) 'Finding a voice', in CAMPLING, J. (Ed) *Images of Ourselves: Women with Disabilities Talking*, London, Routledge and Kegan Paul.

MASON, M. (1992), *Disability Equality in the Classroom: A Human Rights Issue*, London, Disability Equality Publications.

MASON, M. (1994) in MASON, M. and RIESER, R. (Eds) *Altogether Better*, London Comic Relief.

MELLOR, D. (1983) 'If you don't read . . .', in MELLOR, D., *Where Do We Go from Here: Adult Lives without Literacy*, Manchester, Manchester Gatehouse Project.

NABUZOKA, D. (1993) 'Bullying and children with special needs in school', in TATTUM, D. (Ed) *Understanding and Managing Bullying*, London, Heinemann.

RUSSELL, P. and WERTHEIMER, A. (in press) *Something to Say? Groupwork with Young Women with Learning Disabilities*, London, National Children's Bureau.

SSI (SOCIAL SERVICES INSPECTORATE) (1994) *Services to Disabled Children and their Families: Report of the National Inspection of Services for Disabled Children and their Families*, London, HMSO.

THOMAS, A.P., BAX, M. and SMYTH, D.P.L. (1989) *The Health and Social Needs of Young Adults with Physical Disabilities*, London, MacKeith Press.

WADE, B. and MOORE, M. (1993) *Experiencing Special Education*, Milton Keynes, Open University Press.

# 8    Listening To and Communicating With Young Children

*Gillian Pugh and Dorothy Rouse Selleck*

If there is some truth in the general adage that 'children should be seen but not heard', it certainly describes many of our attitudes towards children under the age of six or seven. Whilst many of those working with families and young children may console themselves with the thought that they are now working (or attempting to work) in partnership with parents and that therefore they are more responsive to the needs of children, this both assumes that the partnership has achieved a real shift in the balance of power between parents and professionals, and that parents' voices and rights will be identical to children's voices and rights. These are dangerous assumptions, and in this chapter we will attempt to do three things:

(a)    to ask whether we have a culture in this country that enables us to listen to young children and take their voice seriously;

(b)    to look at some examples of where adults have been able to enter the world of childhood and where opportunities have been created for children to participate and contribute their voice as interdependent members of their families and communities;

(c)    and finally to examine the kind of knowledge and understanding that adults require if they are to develop the skills needed to respect, to listen, to observe and to see and to hear the voice of the child.

## A Culture for Listening to Young Children?

Because young children are particularly vulnerable and dependent on their parents and carers for love and protection, for shelter, food, health care and education, it has been all too easy to see them as appendages or chattels of their parents, and to presume that their needs are subsumed within those of the family. The powerful role that adults living and working with young children play during these formative years has been re-emphasized by a growing public debate about the critical importance of the first five years of a child's life in relation to all aspects of human development. Although the vast majority of these adults — parents, educators and carers — will have the best interests of young children at heart, does this mean that they are really listening to what the children say? Do we, in the multi-cultural society that is Britain, believe that young children should have a voice? Or does mummy/daddy/granny/child care expert always know best, and are we perhaps reluctant to view young children as people with ideas, feelings and contributions of their own even if they may be too young to voice them directly? Do these well meaning 'parent voices' instinctively overrule a more empathetic and informed adult perspective which can give children a chance to talk to us not only through what they say but through their play, their drawings, their actions, and all the subtle ways in which very young children represent their opinions and feelings?

Over the last decade there has been an increasing acceptance that children have rights that are separate from those of their parents and that whilst parents have responsibilities for ensuring their children's rights and needs are met, they may not in all circumstances act in children's best interests. The main impetus for reassessing the status of children in all matters that concern them has been the UN Convention on the Rights of the Child, adopted by the UN General Assembly in 1989 and ratified by the UK government in December 1991. Article 18 of the Convention acknowledges the responsibilities that parents have for the upbringing of their children and recognizes that the best interests of their children will be their primary concern. Article 5 states that governments must 'respect the responsibilities, rights and duties of parents . . . to provide . . . *in a manner consistent with the child's evolving capacity* . . . appropriate direction and guidance in the exercise by the child of the rights' (our italics). Parents' rights are thus seen clearly in the context of the best interests of their children, and account must be taken of the child's evolving capacity.

One issue on which parents' rights are still seen to be in conflict with children's rights is that of physical punishment. As Newell argues (1994) the physical punishment of children within the family remains a hidden problem, often culturally and socially approved. Children's rights to physical integrity — to protection from all forms of inter-personal violence — exist in very few societies, and certainly not in the UK where in 1994, in a much publicized case, a childminder won the right to smack children in her charge, provided she had parental consent.

The Convention is also explicit about listening to the views of children. Article 12 states that every child 'who is capable of forming his or her own views' must have the right 'to express those views freely in all matters affecting the child' and that the views of the child should be 'given due weight in accordance with the age and maturity of the child'. In a society that is not used to giving weight to the views of children of any age, we will need to be strong advocates in minute particulars if children without the voice of mature language users are to be listened to and taken account of. 'Listening' to very young children does not necessarily mean taking all their utterances at face value, but it does mean observing the nuances of how they exhibit stress, or curiosity or anxiety, or pleasure in a manner which is congruent to their maturity. It does not imply that their views carry more weight than the powers of wise and loving adults over the outcome of any decision making process but it does require that their views are respected. As Lansdown points out (1994) this simple and self-evidently worthy principle — that children should be accepted as people in their own right — would, if taken seriously, have a revolutionary impact on the nature of adult/child relationships in this country.

The central concern of the Convention with the welfare and the best interests of children may at times, and particularly in the case of young children, be in conflict with their right to be listened to. The younger the child, the more difficult it will be to place a greater emphasis on self-determination and autonomy than on safety and welfare. One very obvious example of this is the extent to which parents feel able to let their children go out on their own in an increasingly hostile environment. For example, in 1971 some 86 per cent of primary school children went to school on their own; in 1990 it was only 29 per cent, and there have been correspondingly large drops in the number of children allowed to cross roads or ride bikes on their own (Hillman, 1990). Creating situations which allow even younger children to take acceptable risks — playing on the pavement outside the house or in a neighbouring garden for example — presents parents and carers with a very real challenge at the end of the twentieth century.

Moving from the international to the national context, the same conflict is inherent in the 1989 Children Act which enshrines many of the principles of the UN Convention. Built on the principle of the welfare of the child being paramount, it requires that courts and social service departments and education departments in respect of supervision orders take account of the wishes and feelings of children when decisions are made that affect them. But it does not require parents to take account of the views and feelings of children within the family, and neither does it go beyond the relatively small group of children who are the concern of the welfare system. The Scottish Children Bill, going through parliament in 1995, however does require parents to ascertain the views of children on major decisions that affect them. Other public services which have a profound impact on the lives of children — particularly education and health — are under no obligation to either consult with children or to encourage their participation (Newell, 1991).

To find broader statutory regulations regarding listening to young children, we must turn to Denmark, a country that has taken the UN convention very seriously and where leaflets have been distributed to all school children informing them of their rights. Children themselves have contributed to the writing of these leaflets, and summarize Article 12 as 'Children have a right to their own opinion, which must be respected' (Danish Ministry of Social Affairs, 1991). The government has also set up a 'children as citizens' project as a more direct way of listening to and including children. In a country where responsibility for early childhood services has been decentralized, it is also interesting that the State has nevertheless regulated that all children must be listened to and that

children should be included in the planning and execution of activities in daytime childcare facilities, according to their age and maturity, and that children in this way are able to gain experience of the connection between influence and responsibility on a personal and social level. (Danish Ministry of Social Affairs, 1990, Chapter 2)

As a commentator on the Danish experience points out, if we want to listen to children we must create the structures and procedures for making this happen, but

> more important is the cultural climate which shapes the ideas that adults in a particular society hold about children. The wish to listen to and involve children originates in this cultural climate. This wish will then lead to structures and procedures that can guarantee with involvement of children. (Langsted, 1994, pp.41–2)

We would argue that in the UK our structures, procedures and climate are as yet too limited to enable us to take seriously our responsibilities for listening to the voices of young children. There are however some examples of ways in which adults are enabled to enter the world of childhood, and in which children are enabled to play a more equal part in the world of adults, and we examine some of these in the pages which follow.

### Enabling Young Children to Speak

Although most infants do not learn to talk until their second year, their 'voices' are there for us to hear from birth. The importance of close relationships between the baby and the mother and one or two 'key' carers, has been a central part of the child care literature since the early work of Bowlby and Ainsworth, but the way in which very small babies are able to initiate these relationships and set the pace of the 'dance' of interaction between themselves and adults has received rather less attention. The work of Trevarthen (1977, 1995), for example, based on precisely structured tests, shows us that children can have a voice from birth onwards when their mothers can support them 'to speak'.

> *Very young subjects* have consistently exhibited preferences for physical constellations that . . . are unambiguous signs of persons attempting communication . . . Exchanges between two-months-olds and their mothers tend to be precisely patterned in time. The nature of the patterning shows that it is a mutually generated effect, in which the intentions of both partners are essential, and both may adjust their acts to obtain better fit to those of each other. (1977, p.234)

Trevarthen believes that communications at this stage are essentially conversation-like exchanges which are elaborate forms of joint action between the infant and the mother where the infant is the leading partner. He concludes that he has strong evidence that personal relationships, or 'attachments', are contingent upon babies sharing and co-operating. He also argues (1995) that children's communications are both imitative and creative, and describes how every aspect of their cognitive activity is open to qualification by what other people feel and do.

The importance of attachment between parents and children as an essential launch pad for children's ability to have and develop 'a voice' is also described by Leach (1994):

> The spiralling strands of development that transform helpless newborns into sociable and socialised small people are plaited into their relationships with known, loved and loving adults . . . infants need to have permanence, continuity, passion and a parent-like commitment. (p.83)

Leach argues that any kind of personal indifference can be damaging to the developing voices of babies. 'Every time her sounds, expressions and body language are noticed and answered . . . a tiny piece is added to the foundations of that baby's self-esteem, self-confidence and social competence.' These conditions are essential for a child's psycho-social and cognitive growth as well as for their physical well-being and health. Babies, for instance, have to be in control of the feeding process if breast feeding is to be successful. As babies suck at the breast the mother's brain is stimulated to produce the hormones which in turn stimulates the breasts to produce more milk. In other words the baby's voice (the rate and frequency of the sucking) ensures just the right amount of milk. 'Mothers not only do not need to exercise control over their babies suckling, they ruin the process if they do' (Leach, 1994, p.58).

For very young children physical 'relationship play' between adults and children, such as cradling, rocking, supporting and rolling, creating tunnels and rowing the boat, provides nonverbal means of communicating with children. This play can give children a voice to express and manage controlling and being controlled, as well as offering intimacy and closeness. These voices are necessary if small people with less physical strength or power are to develop a sense of their own physical control and integrity and the tools or voice to protect them from adults who use their powers abusively rather than lovingly (Goldschmied and Jackson, 1994). These physical games are also an effective way of increasing children's vocabulary, since words associated with physical experience are more likely to be absorbed and remembered.

The sensitivity to children's feelings and awareness of their social and emotional as well as their cognitive needs must also inform the curriculum offered to young children in day care and nursery school settings. We use 'curriculum' in its broadest sense to include all the opportunities for learning and development that are made available to children; the activities, attitudes and behaviour that are planned, encouraged, tolerated, ignored or forbidden; and the part adults take in organizing, directing, influencing and joining in what the children do (Drummond, Lally and Pugh, 1989).

Children need a curriculum which encourages them to think, choose, plan, challenge and feel valued, to articulate what they think and express how they feel. A curriculum which encourages children to be problem solvers, decision makers and to be independent in their thinking is more likely to give children the success, self-esteem and resilience that Sylva and Wiltshire (1993) argue young children need in order to shape positive attitudes towards themselves.

> The most important learning in pre-school concerns aspirations, task commitment, social skills and responsibility and feelings of efficacy. (p.37)

Although Sylva cites the High/Scope curriculum in support of her argument, arguing that the 'plan, do, review cycle is the cause of greater autonomy, commitment and aspirations' (in Ball, 1994), much of the curriculum thinking currently informing the work of nurseries in the UK provides young children with similar experiences. Athey (1990) for example describes an ideology for the 'know why' of the conceptual understanding of children that comes from study and reflection. Teachers who have listened to the voices of children by systematically observing the patterns in their representation through play, talk, art and actions may identify their 'schema' or, in other words, have a more informed insight into the thinking and ideas communicated to us through the symbolism of their actions. She argues that 'all teachers who listen [to the voice] of children know that there is many a slip between what is offered and what is received' (p.43). Only by careful and informed 'child watching' and listening to the languages in children's play, and then identifying patterns of persistent concerns, will we really be able to pay attention to the voices of children, who have the right to demand a developmentally relevant pedagogy.

In observing and listening to children, it is important to respect and value the cultural heritages of the children and the families and communities from which they come. The Children Act requires us to take account of children's race, language, culture and religion in the provision that we make for them, and it will be easier to listen to young bilingual learners if schools and nurseries employ bilingual staff who can share stories and experiences with the children in their home languages as they settle into school. Cross-cultural research reminds us that children's voices are nurtured in the context of cultural values and expectations. Tobin *et al.* (1989), for example, describe the different ways in which children in China, Japan and America are allowed to use language to express themselves. In Chinese pre-schools the emphasis is on enunciation, diction and the flawless delivery of recitations, stories and songs which express what is socially shared. Children in Japanese schools are allowed two voices, a formal and an informal one. Children are actively indulged to voice their ideas loudly or with as much vulgarity as they please, but this unrestrained voice alternates with periods of polite, formal greetings, blessings and thanks. American children are taught the rules and conventions of self-expression and free speech. In China and the United States, where successful communication is believed to depend largely on the clarity of expression of the speaker, the emphasis is on

teaching children to express themselves clearly, whereas in Japan, where successful communication is believed to depend largely on the empathetic and intuitive
abilities of the listener, children are not so much encouraged to have a voice
of their own but to be sensitive to others' spoken and unspoken forms of self-
expression. Whilst British nurseries will reflect the dominant ideology of the
communities they serve, just as the nurseries in Japan, China and America do,
it is salutary to reflect on the breadth of languages and cultures that will be
represented in communities in the UK.

Tobin *et al.*'s study explores the concept of 'Kodomorashii kodomo', a
Japanese expression used to describe the child-like qualities of very young
people. As well as helping children to be citizens and take their place in communities by enabling them to fit in with and find a place in an adult world, even
more important is for adults to find a way to access the world of childhood.
Young children are more creative and advanced in their thinking than many
adults give them credit for and the skilful adult — whether parent, educator/
teacher, social worker or health worker — is able through observation and
listening to gain real insight into children's preoccupations, thoughts and feelings. Young children are well able to voice their ideas, listen to each others'
ideas, and question and comment on them. Drummond (1993) for example
describes discussions in a classroom between children aged from four to seven.
The curriculum planned for these children and the mutually dependent and
responsive interactions of this teacher with her class releases a stream of imaginative associations, humour and beautiful images. She is able to nurture children's
ability to sort through their experience, and reclassify it in new and unexpected
ways. Drummond suggests that

> there are unlimited opportunities [in discussion groups] to see important
> and worthwhile aspects of learning: children listening, collaborating,
> agreeing and disagreeing; children thinking logically and imaginatively,
> connectedly and with sudden flashes of insight; children using simile
> and metaphor; children moving from the concrete example to the abstract
> formulation; children recognizing causal and functional relationships,
> making generalizations and qualifications; children's humour and origin-
> ality; children learning the purposes of the act of discussion itself, and
> their own powers to contribute to it. (p.62)

Exploration of the moral dimensions of loneliness and rejection as children learn
social skills and manage the fears and pleasures of peer group play are at the heart
of Vivian Paley's kindergarten classroom. In her book *You can't say you can't play*
(1992) she describes ways in which she enables children to share their view of
the world not only by careful observation and sensitive listening, but by her
teacher's art of story telling. With stories specially created for her children she
weaves a fantasy about a magpie which transforms dreams and memories; anxieties of exclusion; and the powerful feelings of efficacy and control that come
from being an initiator and leader (I'm the king of the castle . . . you're the dirty

rascal). In her society of the classroom, which is a microcosm of society at large, this teacher understands the power of imagination and symbolism in stories that can open up discussions with young children. In her classroom they are able to attack the evils of exclusion, inequality and meanness and find ways to weave goodness, respect and sensitivity into the voices of young children learning to live and learn symbiotically in groups.

In the account of *The Boy Who Would Be a Helicopter*, Paley reminds us that there is a tendency to look upon the noisy, repetitive fantasies of children as 'non-educational', but helicopters and super heroes are story telling aids and conversational tools, particularly for children who are distressed or withdrawn. 'Without them, the range of what we listen to and talk about is arbitrarily circumscribed by the adult point of view' (Paley, 1990, p.39).

## Observing Children's Non-verbal Communication

For adults, voicing friendships and sharing ideas can be expressed through language. Words which are parts of conversations are used to argue, to negotiate, to make arrangements, to express ambivalence or enthusiasm, rage or conciliation, affection or impatience. Young children's interactions often have a different voice.

Listening to young children through observing their play and talking about their drawings has a particular significance for those working with children who have been abused and neglected or traumatized. Social workers and therapists must employ a wide range of skills and techniques to build up a trusting relationship with children who may have had few consistent relationships in their lives, or experienced frequent rejection. Play is a powerful means of developing a relationship with a child and providing opportunities to observe the child's concerns and preoccupations, whether demonstrated explicitly or implicitly. But it is important that the time, space, resources and professional skills are available if workers are both to observe accurately what the child is 'saying' to them, and are to be able to follow up what they observe. Thurgood (1990) argues that the success of any attempt to listen to children depends on the worker becoming a sufficiently reliable and consistent figure in the child's world. 'Each child needs to be treated as an individual and to have the experience of adults recognizing and ideally enjoying this individuality' (p.58).

Ensuring that familiar people provide continuity of care in communicating with distressed children is also emphasized by Richman (1993), on the basis of her experiences in Mozambique with children affected by war. 'This is especially important for young children who find it very difficult to trust and communicate with someone unfamiliar' (p.14). She argues that from birth children are very sensitive to the emotional climate around them, and though they cannot put their feelings into words they do express themselves through dreams and nightmares, wakefulness at night, losing their tempers, their play and drawings. Richman emphasizes that very young children are aware of the distress of other people and are affected by dangerous or sad experiences. Adults need to give explanations for curfews and violence, and to explain absence of family members through death or detention. Children need to be allowed a 'voice' to express their grief or confusion and to be comforted and informed about who is going to take care of them. Richman shares her knowledge of the cultural differences in giving advice and comfort and reminds us that it is important to use ways of helping children that are appropriate to their particular culture. Coping strategies for managing stress through the voices of drama, music and story making are also used in inner city nurseries to help staff and children cope with the racial tension and family pressures (Lahad, 1992).

The importance of taking rich fantasy play seriously instead of dismissing weapons and noisy activities as bad behaviour or problems is also stressed by Whalley in her work in a nursery (1994). Observation of the patterns in children's play so that educators can understand children's current obsessions (or 'schema') enables parents and staff to listen to children thinking and learning, rather than dismiss their behaviour as lacking in purpose, concentration, or as being obstreperous.

We can also listen to children through talking about their pictures. In discussing young children's mark making, Dawn and Fred Sedgwick (1993) quote the mother of a four year old who was looking back at her daughter's drawings over two or three years:

> You can see the development. There are a couple of really eerie ones, and maybe they show what she was thinking; when you're having another baby for example. In one drawing she was about three, the round figures look like lost souls. And she said 'I'm lost and I'm saying help me, help me . . . I don't like the ones you orchestrate!' When you leave them alone they're the best ones . . . their perceptions get on to the paper. (p.15)

As the authors point out, this mother did have an active role in the creation of the drawings, by encouraging, enabling, finding tools, time and space. They then go on to look at mark-making in the nursery, arguing that artistic work with children for whom English is not a first language is particularly worthwhile 'as it offers a valuable release for emotions which cannot be articulated and it is a means of communicating with other children'.

In longitudinal studies of his own children from birth to adulthood Matthews (1994) interprets the meanings of children's movements, their drawings and paintings, and then addresses the relationship between graphic representation and play, speech, writing, and spatial or mathematical skills. In the following observation which combines the perceptions of the besotted involvement of a loving father with the precise descriptions of the researcher he invites us to listen and to enter the world of the child-like communications of children:

> At four days old, as I bend over her while she lies on her back, Hannah makes rhythmical arm and leg movements towards me. The movements

are almost circular, alternating from one arm to another. Each movement is a little like a crawl swimming stroke. This kind of behaviour
is called a synergistic response. The same can be observed when children begin to paint and draw . . . early drawing and painting involve
many movements, not only those of the drawing hand. It is as though
the children are acting out an internal description, story, event or image
they had in their minds. (p.33)

People who take time to watch the conversational dances of young children
may be privileged to glimpse their minds and meanings.

Symbolism may also be seen through physical representation, where intro-
ducing children to a range of symbol systems frees them to voice their ideas in
new and exciting ways. The long jump project of three to six year olds in
Reggio Emilia (Forman, 1993) began with the physical drama of acting out the
photographs of Olympic long jumpers and went on to encompass every kind
of representation, using a rich provision of media and symbolism, verbal discussions, graphics, mimicry and gestures.

The graphics and gestures help the children communicate their diver-
gent ideas, and the verbal dialogue will help them reach a consensus
(p.172) . . . The 'Hundred Languages of Children' . . . has been interpreted to mean that all children learn best when they can learn multiple
symbol systems to understand complex relations. (p.188)

### Children Learning to be Citizens: A Role in Decision Making

Our discussion so far has focused on adults observing and listening to the voices
of children so as to better understand their world. But, to return to the principles of the UN Convention and the 1989 Children Act, it is also important
to create a society in which young children are treated with respect and dignity
and in which they can begin to take their place as citizens. In small ways this
is happening in nurseries, schools, clinics and hospitals across the country. Whalley
(1994), for example, describes how in creating an environment at Pen Green
nursery in which children could learn

. . . our primary concern was with the development of self-esteem in
children. It was enshrined in our curriculum document . . .
Children should feel strong
Children should feel in control
Children should feel able to question
Children should feel able to choose. (p.26)

Of course Whalley does not imply that nurseries or classrooms should be controlled by children. Children certainly need to feel strong and in control, but
they also need to be certain that adults are still responsible for creating firm

boundaries with which they can feel safe and protected. Commenting on the importance of routines, a parent at Pen Green writes

> ... the children who were the least settled in nursery were those whose routine was upset and those children who were not getting a chance to control their lives in any way. (p.101)

As Whalley comments

> ... there are still important patterns to the day and important boundaries to be set down in nurseries like ours where children are encouraged to be decision makers and human rights negotiators. (p.162)

At a time when the debate about what is a quality service for young children is gathering momentum, we would suggest that children have as much right to contribute to this debate as parents, staff, inspectors and the government. It is now becoming more common for children and young people to be involved in discussions about school policy, but this does not always include the nursery age children. Sue Mulvaney, head of Kexborough Primary School thought it important to involve the whole school (from the nursery upwards) in discussions about the schools equal opportunities policy, about the playground rules and the work rules, and in answering the question 'what kind of school do we want?' This is the charter the children drew up:

> We want our school to be a place where
>   –hidden talents are revealed
>   –there is lots of choice
>   –teachers ask you for your opinion
>   –there are smiling faces
>   –people tell the truth
>   –no-one gets left out
>   –you can trust others
>   –you are trusted
>   –children come because they enjoy it
>   –we work together, for each other — a big team
>   –all pupils are given opportunities, not just one or two
>   –pupils are prepared for their next school
>   –it is clean and tidy and well-looked after
>   –there are exciting things to do and children work hard
>   –there is a place for playing.

Reflecting on these two projects, Newson comments

> While children involved in decision making may grow up to expect more participation in society, there is always the risk that we will have given them cause to be disillusioned by the democratic process by the

age of eight. Yes children should be heard. Are we also prepared to listen? (p.11) Similar examples come from the Patio estate in Swinton in South Yorkshire where children aged between three and eight were involved in replanning the estate and presenting their views to Rotherham councillors; and a play project in Swansea where children under five were involved in replanning playgrounds (Newson, 1995).

Many examples of good practice in the field of early childhood care and education come from elsewhere in Europe. For example, Langsted (1994) describes a project in Denmark where staff working with children between the ages of six months and three years reviewed the rules and tried to give the children more of a say in what happened. The 'Children as Citizens' project noted above involved thirteen and fourteen year olds who studied the children in a kindergarten for two days and then met with staff and parents to discuss ways of giving young children more of a say in the running of the nursery — for example why should all the children go out to play at the same time rather than when they wanted to?

Langsted also describes a project in which five year old children were interviewed about their daily lives. Although there are problems of reliability and validity in interviewing young children, Langsted and his colleagues in Norway, Sweden, Finland, Iceland and Denmark have devised a system for studying the lives of 123 five year olds, through interviews and observations. As part of this study twenty-four kindergarten children were asked about the quality of their kindergarten — the presence of other children was the most important factor in determining quality for them, with activities, toys and nice staff of secondary importance. The children were also very aware of the different rules at home and in the centre, and the different levels of self-determination that were possible and they were quite able to function in both systems. The examples cited by Langsted show that 'even young children have strong opinions about their everyday life, and there is evidence that you can improve the life conditions of children by listening and going along with their opinions'.

On a visit to Reggio Emilia in Northern Italy, we observed that particular attention had been given to the design and the arrangement of the equipment in the day nurseries to enable even the youngest children to have a say in the decisions of routine, pace and control that they had over their environment. For example cots, or 'nests' as the staff called them, were made like baskets and were placed at floor level. As soon as babies can crawl they can choose the comfort of their personal nest without being reliant on adults to hoist them in and out of an inaccessible cage on stilts, which is the tradition in most nurseries. These babies could also collect their own clean nappy from low cupboards and choose to climb on a little ramp up to changing mats where they were able to invite adults to change them. This autonomy and control was teaching children about their own rights to privacy, about the integrity of their own bodies, and their right to choose which key people that they felt most close to, and familiar with, that they wanted to take care of their intimate needs. How different from our observations in some nurseries where powerless babies and toddlers are collected like parcels and expected to submit to cleaning and changing routines at the hand of the next staff member on the duty rota who changes all the babies in turn at a pre-set time! With imagination and a commitment to a policy of respect for the sensibilities and 'voices' of children, the Italian nursery had built an environment and a way of communicating with babies that allowed for reciprocity, and minimized autocratic or manipulative interactions from the more powerful adults (Rouse, 1992).

To return to the UK and to the field of health care, an example of respecting the ability of young children to make decisions and enabling them to do so comes from the Hospital for Sick Children, Great Ormond Street, London. Here the introduction of patient-controlled analgesia (PCA) (which allows the patient to control the level of analgesia he or she receives according to the levels of discomfort) has been extended for use with children as young as four — or at whatever age the child is able to understand the relationship between using the triggering device and receiving medicine which will make them feel less sore (Llewellyn, 1993). 'Action for Sick Children' has, for many years, been working to help young children be prepared for and cope with the challenges of a stay in hospital and possible surgery. Their leaflet on *Children and Pain* emphasizes the importance of listening to children when making decisions about pain control.

From a legal and social work perspective, the Children Act requires the courts in many cases, including inter-parental disputes, to have regard to the 'ascertainable wishes and feelings of the child concerned (considered in the light of his (sic) age and understanding)'. Yet the court cannot have regard to these feelings and wishes unless it can discover what they are — by listening to the child, and the mechanisms for discovering the child's views are inconsistent. For example, the guardian ad litem system available in care cases is not normally available in private family cases.

As far as children being accepted as competent witnesses is concerned, although a Court of Appeal ruling in 1990 said that there is no magic age below which a child is automatically disqualified from giving evidence, according to Lord Chief Justice Lane it is up to the judge trying the case to decide whether the particular child in question is 'of sufficient intelligence to justify the reception of the evidence and understands the duty of speaking the truth' (Spencer, 1990). He added that a child of five would come up to the required standard 'very rarely'. As Spencer argues, in most other legal systems, including Scotland, the courts are willing in principle to listen to the evidence of children virtually from the age that they can talk. 'If this can be done north of the Tweed it is hard to think of any sane reason why we cannot do it here' (p.115).

## Enabling Adults to Listen

Children are entitled to live and learn with adults who understand how children develop and who accept and respect them as young people in their own right, and know how to listen to them. They are also entitled to live in a society which respects their right to be listened to and to participate in decisions which affect their lives. The examples of good practice that we have summarized in this chapter require sensitivity and empathy on the part of adults — parents and carers as well as professional workers — but they also require changes in many of the institutions in which young children spend some of their lives.

The skills and attitudes that adults will require include:

(a) expectations of children which are appropriate to their stage of development and level of understanding;

(b) the ability to listen reflectively so that consideration is given to assessment and to planning opportunities. This kind of reflective listening will allow for time and space, and developmentally appropriate possibilities, for giving small children a voice;

(c) the ability to see things from the child's point of view;

(d) the ability to observe and interpret their representations, to appreciate the significance of their play, their movements, their art and music as powerful child-like voices of communications;

(e) the ability to extend children's thinking, and to build up conversational reciprocal exchanges which open up opportunities for them to communicate their ideas, thoughts and feelings. Children need the experience and practice of listening, reflecting, questioning, negotiating, asking and answering, predicting and recalling. These skills will need to be modelled and supported by adults if they are to give children their voice;

(f) the ability to be respectful, accepting and patient. Adults need to be able to use their powers wisely and responsibly to give children positive feedback on how they can be more successful or effective. Children do not need empty or patronising praise, but appreciation related explicitly and directly to what they are interested in and the effort that they have put in (Katz, 1993). They have a right to factual and informative criticism so that they can learn how to develop their voice in all kinds of relationships (Drummond, Rouse and Pugh, 1992);

(g) the ability to help children express and manage their feelings, and not to negate feelings of fear or anger. Adults need to be able to hear children's voices of resistance and protest. If we are to hear and respond honestly to all children's' emotions and wishes then we need to listen to children's' angry voices too. Half a century ago the Polish paediatrician Janusz Korczak advocated that:

> The child has the right to resist educational influence that conflicts with his or her own beliefs. It is fortunate for mankind that we are unable to force children to yield to assaults upon their common sense and humanity. The child has the right to protest at injustice (in Lifton, 1989, from the Appendix).

These are some of the skills and attitudes that are required by all who live and work with young children, and attention should be paid to them in the education and support offered to parents and prospective parents (Pugh *et al.*, 1994) and in the training courses of all professionals. It is a cause of considerable concern that the study of child development is now an insignificant part of initial teacher training, despite research which shows that teachers and other early childhood workers cite this as the most important part of their training (Blenkin and Yue, 1994).

But there are implications too for the way in which institutions are organized. In her book *Child Protection and Early Years Teachers* (1993) David describes the ethos of the 'listening school'. Whilst she admits that the first step in developing such a school — a recognition of a child's right to be heard — demands an enormous step in attitudinal change, it is possible to devise strategies towards a listening school, not unlike those developed at Pen Green and at Kexborough school above. Such strategies (which could equally be applied to hospitals, clinics, or any centres or groups in which young children were to be found or, with adaptation, to families) might begin from questions such as

(a)   who has a voice in decision making (governors, all teachers, parents, children, support staff?)
(b)   do young children have the information they need to participate in decision-making?
(c)   if children are involved, how are their voices heard?
(d)   do all members of staff have appropriate skills and understanding of child development, and the ability to observe and to listen?
(e)   are they committed to taking children's views seriously?
(f)   is there a role for designated staff to have a cross-school brief for listening to children's views and to be advocates for children? Such staff could have responsibility for interpreting decisions or proposals from a child's point of view, which could be a formal and necessary part of any decision making process that would affect young children.
(g)   how is the school organized? is there space and is there time for children to talk to teachers if they want to?

Listening to, communicating with and involving young children requires a cultural climate that understands children and takes them seriously. Laws, structures and procedures are important, but only if as a society we want the climate to change. The examples that we have cited show that change is possible, but they are the exception rather than the rule. If the voices of young children are to be heard it will need more than a few gifted and dedicated parents and professionals to hear them.

# References

ACTION FOR SICK CHILDREN (1992) *Children and Pain*, London, Action for Sick Children.

ATHEY, C. (1990) *Extending Thought in Young Children*, London, Paul Chapman Publishing.

BLENKIN, G. and YUE, N. (1994) 'Profiling early years practitioners: Some first impressions from a national survey', *Early Years* **15**, 1, pp.13–22.

DANISH MINISTRY OF SOCIAL AFFAIRS (1990) *Government Circular 203 Concerning Child Care for Children and Young People According to the Danish Public Assistance Act*, Copenhagen.

DANISH MINISTRY OF SOCIAL AFFAIRS AND DANISH UNICEF COMMITTEE (1991) *Convention on the Rights of Children*, Copenhagen.

DAVID, T. (1993) *Child Protection and Early Years Teachers*, Milton Keynes, Open University Press.

DRUMMOND, M.J. (1993) *Assessing Children's Learning*, London, David Fulton.

DRUMMOND, M.J., LALLY, M. and PUGH, G. (1989) *Working with Children; Developing a Curriculum in the Early Years*, London, National Children's Bureau/NES Arnold.

DRUMMOND, M.J., ROUSE, D. and PUGH, G. (1992) *Making Assessment Work*, London, National Children's Bureau/NES Arnold.

EDWARDS, C., GANDINI, L. and FORMAN, G. (Eds) (1993) *The Hundred Languages of Children: The Reggio Emilia Approach to Early Childhood Education*, New Jersey, Ablex Publishing.

FORMAN, G. (1993) 'Multiple symbolization in the long jump project', in EDWARDS, C., GANDINI, L. and FORMAN, G. (Eds) *The Hundred Languages of Children: the Reggio Emilia Approach to Early Childhood Education*, New Jersey, Ablex Publishing Co.

GOLDSCHMIED, E. and JACKSON, S. (1994) *People Under Three: Young Children in Day Care*, London, Routledge.

HILLMAN, J., ADAMS, J. and WHITELEGG, J. (1990) *One False Move: A Study of Children's Independent Mobility*, London, Policy Studies Institute.

KATZ, L.G. (1993) 'Are we confusing self-esteem and narcissism?', *Young Children*, November, 2–3.

LAHAD, M. (1992) 'Story making in assessment, method for coping with stress', in JENNINGS, S. (Ed) *Dramatherapy. Theory and Practice*, London, Tavistock/Routledge.

LANGSTED, O. (1994) 'Looking at quality from the child's perspective', in MOSS, P. and PENCE, A. (Eds) *Valuing Quality in Early Childhood Services*, London, Paul Chapman.

LANSDOWN, G. (1994) 'Children's rights and the under eights', *Coordinate*, May, pp.7–11.

LEACH, P. (1994) *Children First*, London, Michael Joseph.

LIFTON, B.J. (1989) *The King of Children*, London, Pan Books.

LLEWELLYN, N. (1993) 'The use of PCA for paediatric post-operative pain management', *Paediatric Nursing*, **5**, 5, pp.12–15.

MATTHEWS, J. (1994) *Helping Children to Draw and Paint in Early Childhood, Children and Visual Representation*, Sevenoaks, Hodder and Stoughton.

NEWELL, P. (1991) *The UN Convention and Children's Rights in the UK*, London, National Children's Bureau.

NEWELL, P. (1994) *The Child's Right to Physical and Personal Integrity within the Family in Europe*, London, Epoch Worldwide.

NEWSON, E. (1995) 'The patio project', *Coordinate*, January, pp.10–11.

PALEY, V.G. (1990) *The Boy Who Would Be A Helicopter*, Boston, Harvard University Press.

PALEY, V.G. (1992) *You Can't Say You Can't Play*, Boston, Harvard University Press.

PUGH, G., DE'ATH, E. and SMITH, C. (1994) *Confident Parents, Confident Children: policy and practice in parent education and support*, London, National Children's Bureau.

RICHMAN, N. (1993) *Communicating with Children. Helping Children in Distress*, London, Save the Children.

ROUSE, D. (1992) *The Italian Experience*, London, National Children's Bureau. (Unpublished paper)

SEDGWICK, D. and SEDGWICK, F. (1993) *Drawing to Learn*, Sevenoaks, Hodder and Stoughton.

SPENCER, J.R. (1990) 'Persuading the courts to listen to children', in BANNISTER, A., BARRETT, K. and SHEARER, E. (Eds) *Listening to Children: The Professional Response to Hearing the Abused Child*, London, Longman.

SYLVA, K. and WILTSHIRE, J. (1993) 'The impact of early learning on later development', *European Early Childhood Education Research Journal*, **1**, 1, pp.17–40.

SYLVA, K. (1994) 'A curriculum for early learning', in BALL, C. *Start Right. The Importance of Early Learning*, London, Royal Society of Arts.

THURGOOD, J. (1990) 'Active listening — a social service's perspective', in BANNISTER, A., BARRETT, K. and SHEARER, E. (Eds) *Listening to Children: The Professional Response to Hearing the Abused Child*, London, Longman.

TOBIN, J.J., WU, D.Y.H. and DAVIDSON, D.H. (1989) *Preschool in Three Cultures*, London, Yale University Press.

TREVARTHEN, C. (1977) 'Descriptive analysis of infant communicative behaviour', in SCHAFFER, H.R. (Ed) *Studies in Mother Infant Interaction*, London, Academic Press.

TREVARTHEN, C. (1995) 'The child's need to learn a culture', *Children and Society*, **9**, 1, pp.5–19.

WHALLEY, M. (1994) *Learning to be Strong: Setting up a Neighbourhood Service for Under Fives and their Families*, Sevenoaks, Hodder and Stoughton.

# 9 Gender Issues

*Gill Gorell Barnes*

Gender is a powerful organizer of social functioning in children. Once a child understands the categories of gender, they are likely to use this influential classification to organize the way they see and understand events (McAninch *et al.*, 1993). Maccoby (1988) further asserts that gender schema, concepts organizing definitions of what belongs to male and female behaviour, are extremely resistant to change and disconfirmation. Alongside gender, culture, here defined as being the structure of beliefs and habits of living within the child's home, organizes the specific and personal arrangement of gendered expectations unique to each child.

What are likely to be the hazards, then, for professionals meeting children if they have not thought about issues of gender? The first hazard may be that ease of communication will be blocked, not only by the inherent power inequalities involved in any relationship between adult and child, but also by the assumptions a child may have of how a person of the professional's gender and culture should behave, and how they, as a girl or boy, should respond. The second is to do with misunderstandings arising from the professional's lack of awareness about issues from the child's world which are likely to be crucial to the child's own understanding of themselves, and the milieu that is their own. The third hazard is more subtle and will require ongoing monitoring, since it will involve gendered nuances of language; language both between people and within the mind; how a child thinks and does not think; what may not be thought about and what may not be said.

## Family Influences

It may also be crucial for the child to understand that they have permission from the adults of the relevant gender to speak. In many family cultures issues of loyalty are not only specific to child/parent hierarchies, but to being a boy or a girl in that family and that kinship group. If the context of the interview is one where the child is at risk, this will take longer to negotiate as is discussed further below. Older boys and girls who have taken on key gate-keeping functions on behalf of the family, like caring for sibs or an ill parent; or hiding family discordance from a prying world; may be reluctant to engage in processes which they see as disqualifying the protective work they had been doing.

How does gender enter into the interview interactions themselves, as an important dimension? As outlined above, there are always going to be cultural representations of gendered behaviour organizing children's understanding of what is required of them, and these may conflict with what a professional is expecting. Rules about the expected behaviour of girls and of boys will have evolved in the family and then been reinforced, amplified, or a different set of rules taught, within the wider context of school. We must assume that in a new situation a child will not know the rules and expectations about how they as a girl or boy should behave. It is very likely that the professional in turn will not know the gender related rules of the family as they affect the child, so that an important part of any meeting will require slow and patient enquiry, willingness to listen to the child's way of telling, and giving an opportunity for the child to find out how to fit what they know to what is required for the purposes of the meeting.

## The Social Context and Individual Meaning

How does gender, as part of the fabric of family life, become woven into the individual's own meaning about themselves, their own sex and the other sex (Haste, 1987)? Where do these processes take place? One place is mealtimes. Ochs and Taylor (1992) analyzed a hundred meal time conversations within white American families and noted how conversational habits shape the social political dimensions of family life. Mother introduced topics, and controlled their flow, Father was the primary recipient of most of her efforts, but also most often redefined the narratives of other family members in problem-focused ways. Gendered models offered to the boys and girls at these dinner tables would therefore obviously carry particular nuances regarding men and women talking. For many families a daily meal constitutes the place where family members collaboratively establish how relevant events outside the family — at school, at work or in different members' social reference groups — are to be interpreted within the family, and the implications for the different actions of men and women. Acts of co-operation, need meeting, service giving, etc. and the ways in which the family handle these are discussed and decided on. How children come to participate in, as well as perceive, definitions of gendered activity depends on their age, comprehension, and allocated status.

Many families do not eat together daily, but eat at different times of day, or in different family groupings. Some families only sit down together for festivals. However, how human beings interact in the small details of family life like meals reflects the organization of culture, that is wider belief systems as well as social organization. The nuances of such interactions, as well as the hundred other sequences of family life, will affect the children's views of their gendered selves when they are away from the family as well as when they are within it.

## Gender Identity and Family Nuance

Identity, and particularly sexual identity, develops in mutual interaction with the males and females in nuclear and extended families. Intimacy and sexual identity are closely interwoven. The gendered sensitivities of the child's body are interpreted through early experiences in a sexed family world and the meanings the child attaches to these (Jones, 1986), as are their understandings of intimacy, protection, power and abuse (Radke-Yarrow, 1988). Questions of power and the arrangements and constraints related to power are determined not only by the child's direct experience of mother, father and other senior men and women in the family; but by her/his perception of the relationships between all the various relationships over more than one generation (Gorell Barnes and Henesy, 1994). Such patterns, lived and observed over time will all contribute to the child's own gendered self perception and self valuation.

Words will also carry specific nuanced meanings which develop through these multiple cross-joined gendered interactions (see the discussion on love below). Language develops from socialization processes outside children into their inner world (Vygotsky, 1981). Children not only participate in the processes of gendered socialization (live them) but also observe and reflect on those processes as they witness them happening around them. Elsewhere, (Gorell Barnes, 1994) I have argued for an interactional and a socio-cultural approach when examining 'mind'. If we take this view we can also accept that the way in which the nuances of gender are carried will be time, country, district and class specific.

## Frames for Thinking about Children and Gender

How gender can usefully be brought into a professional mind when thinking about working with, or interviewing, boy or girl children is discussed briefly below with reference to three theoretical frames. The first is attachment theory, which offers a way of thinking about the importance of close, intimate relationships throughout life; the second is object relations theory and the third is through the developing work of women writers and therapists, particularly those who have written from the Stone Centre in the USA.

### Attachment Theory

Main *et al.*, (1985) have used the concept of 'internal working models' as a way of explaining how young children represent and construct relationships in their minds. The young child's relationships will be formed out of a long and cumulative experience of their interaction with a parent, (Stern, 1977, 1985) and of their parents' interactions with other people (Radke Yarrow *et al.*, 1988). The mind builds up pictures or schema of a history of interactions and responses, which include over time the feelings that go with these as well as the sense of control or helplessness that the reciprocal sequences of interaction have generated over time (Dowling, 1993). Attachment theorists have proposed that these sequences can be categorized into three major groups, leading to security, to avoidance and to uncertainty. Bowlby argued that there is a biologically based tendency to seek and maintain proximity to an attachment figure, and in studying these patterns over years researchers have concluded that children will develop one of the following models of attachment: (a) Where a caregiver is welcoming and permits access when a child wants it, the infant will develop a secure working model. (b) Where a caregiver does not respond appropriately or refuses access the infant will develop an insecure avoidant working model. (c) If the caregiver permits access but responds in unpredictable or bizarre ways this leads to an insecure ambivalent working model.

### Object Relations Theory: How Do Individuals Mentally Represent their Own Early Relationships with their Parenting Figures?

One aspect of psychoanalytic object relations theory as it applies to infancy and early childhood defines an infant as biologically predisposed to engage with other people. Primitive modes of interpersonal sharing and conflict are mentally represented in the language of object relations (Fairbairn, 1952). Infants register when the person looking after them and interacting with them is not appropriately attuned with and responsive to their state of minds; also demonstrated in interactional research (Stern, 1985; Corboz-Warnery et al., 1993; Murray, 1992). If things go well enough children develop an internal world in which schemata, mental representations and fantasies of self, other relationships, are essentially benign (Fonagy et al., 1991, 1993). On the other hand if early caretaking is inadequate or actively unkind or cruel, powerful feelings that are created come to 'people' the infant's mind. In time these inner people will also be gendered. Men and women will carry anticipated 'loadings' in the child's mind. Where negative inner images persist, uncorrected by improved external relations, they affect over time the potential to evolve positive images of self and other relationships. The capacity to hold a number of different views about the self and others, of either or both genders, may be impaired. As children acquire concepts about the minds of others, their view of these minds may develop increasing complexity or may be channelled by early negative experience into the development of perceptions of self and other which have predominantly negative or fearful patterns excluding other more positive possibilities.

In systemic therapy growing attention is now paid to a similar concept of 'dominant and marginalized voices'. While these can be seen in part as an inner dialogue such voices do not only come from within the individual. They can also be found to be active and ongoing in the family to which the individual remains connected, even when they are well grown. In addition, the wider culture and society 'privileges' certain voices at the expense of others. Human beings may be defined and described in many different ways, but too often one description may become dominant and fixed at the expense of others that recognize other potential. While such 'blaming' can happen particularly powerfully in families, it can also happen in schools where a particular group of children, for different reasons, become marginalized and disqualified as not worthy of further curiosity (Steadman, 1985). Any professional newly engaging with a child offers an opportunity either to 'crystallise' a particular trait as stable; or through interest and curiosity to discover a number of new possibilities in the child. The importance of this second option cannot be over emphasized. Emerging from research showing young people's capacity to change given new chances (Quinton and Rutter, 1984; Rutter, 1989) it also forms the basis of a variety of therapeutic approaches (Andersen, 1992; White and Epston, 1989).

### Emotional processes for boys and girls

Recent reviews have found relatively few differences in the socialization processes of boys and girls within the family (Lytton and Romney, 1991) but there is evidence that the socialization of 'emotion' has marked gender differences. From infancy onwards parents respond differently to anger in boys and girls, responding more negatively to angry behaviour in girls but showing more tolerance and even encouragement to boys. Girls are also ticked off more than boys for failing to show kindness to others or for not behaving unselfishly. These behaviours encouraged or discouraged within the home then become reinforced at school, further shaping ongoing gender differences. Boys fight it out, and girls do not: attempting instead to come to consensus through discussion (Maccoby, 1986; Gilligan, 1982). When it comes to the expression of distress, boys are more likely to blame others, while girls are more likely to blame themselves. This fact, replicated in many studies from quite different theoretical backgrounds, is perhaps one of the key facts for professionals to note, since it will have implications for any piece of work they undertake.

### The Work of Women Writers and Therapists: Developmental Issues for Girls

Women therapists who have written about the development of boys and girls have drawn some important distinctions about their emotional development. In the first stage of life the central goal for an infant of either sex is the development of basic trust in another human being. Baker Miller (1986) has hypothesized that with girl children there is a heightened sense of connectedness to the caregiver. The mental construction of self, while depending on 'security of attachment' as theorised by Bowlby and as outlined above is also thought to develop in girls as a more sensitive awareness of their own part in the process of emotional interplay and therefore in turn as an agent in relationship.

While this early 'interacting sense of self' may well be present for infants of both sexes the culturally induced beliefs of the caretakers about girls and boys plays a part from the moment of birth. Girls on the whole are encouraged to feel and to care about the feelings of others. Boys in western cultures however, are on the whole, diverted from emotionality towards independence and outward resilience.

> the mother scaffolds the child's interpretation of his or her experience in such a way as to provide a framework in which gender is highly salient and which ensures that boys have a different framework to interpreting experience than do girls . . . by thirteen months boys and girls behave differently and are affectively operating on different representation schema. (Lloyd, 1987)

Culture specific variables of these gendered schema are likely to have a myriad different forms, and deserve much greater study in our current British society.

In utilizing any theory that makes a distinction between boys' and girls' emotionality it is also important to remember that some children, who have been under long term stress will have complex models of intimacy that often do not fit any 'norm'. Many children of either gender who have played a part in some way as family caretakers, may be highly sensitised to issues of connectedness to other family members, and may well have played an active part in the protection of others.

## Boys and Girls Dealing with Family Distress

Let us contrast two girls and two boys of the same age both confronting a not uncommon situation for children: their mother taking a new partner, who is not their parent, after a period of living as a single parent. Each is reacting violently in different ways, but in each example the girls' violence is an open expression of her own feared loss of relationship. The boys' behaviour in the home, while involving similar fears, also involves more open acting out of hostility and is in each case more physical and less verbal.

Louisa (aged 11) rang up an agency that she understood to be for children in distress to say that a crisis was threatening her family. It transpired that she did not like the fact that her mother, after nine years of living without a partner, had now found a man she was planning to set up home with. Louisa's sense of panic and fury at the idea of another person entering her mother's emotional world was expressed by her as being 'shut away from her mother'. As the interaction between mother and daughter developed in the interview room, it could be seen how important to her was her role in looking after the mother who had looked after her and her little brother for nine years. 'I've always been grown up. I had to grow up quickly because Daddy left . . . I'm used to being responsible'. She says that in her life nothing is as important as 'looking after Paul and Mum'. 'You've always needed me, and now you don't need me and

I still need you'. She says to the counsellor 'She's always looked after herself and Paul, but in a way I've sort of looked after her too'. Catching onto the power of this important job in the girl's sense of her self and her own identity the counsellor said, 'and it's very sad to think of giving that job up isn't it?' she replies, 'It's because I've been so used to it, it's me, I'm so used to it . . . and then this man comes along and says 'well, I'll take over that job, thank you'.

Anna, aged 7, described a similar sense of exclusion. In describing her mother's current boyfriend she said, 'I've got bad vibes (vibrations) from him'. Due to early experiences of sexual abuse from her own father and a distancing of herself from expressed emotion, she rarely expressed her feelings directly, usually describing them at one remove. Following an indirect question using her own manner of detached speech, 'what did the boyfriend do to her that led to the vibe showing itself?' she replied 'the vibe started to show itself when he started to be nasty to me . . . he started to say things. When I was doing little things for Mum he said he wanted to do everything that was to do with her. It felt like he was pushing me away'. The 'vibe' then was an externalized manifestation of Anna's fear of being separated from the person to whom she was closest in the world, her mother.

To feel more related to another person for a girl then may be to feel oneself enhanced. Boys may be just as closely connected as girls in families where they have been encouraged to be so, or had to 'look after' a parent who has been ill or incapacitated, and just as anxious about these connections being severed. However it is likely that the display of connected behaviour will be tolerated less well by an incoming adult and will be correctly construed as deliberately trying to keep someone else away. Unlike a girl, a boy may be more directly responded to aggressively, and as a rival, by a new male partner. Sean, aged five, came with his stepfather and his mother following a crisis line call initiated by his mother's co-habitee who feared the violence of his own responses to Sean's 'possessive' behaviour of Mum. 'He will not leave you alone, he follows you around like a little dog . . . he pulls and pulls at your arm until its sore, and it's Mum, Mum, Mum'. Mother had previously been left by father, when Sean was eighteen months old and had subsequently been in hospital three times for overdosing. His concern thus had at least two levels of meaning; how his mother would fare with a new man in her life as well as for himself. The advent of a new man raised other questions . . . would a new man coming in mean that he was displaced. Was there only room in the family for one man at a time? (see Cooklin *et al.*, 1994 for a discussion of these issues).

Bob, aged ten, was furious not so much for his loss of his mother who had decided to re-marry, but by this further proof that his mother was not going to return to his father (although they had been living apart for over three years). He had attacked his mother on three occasions, and had also hit his father's girlfriend in the face. 'She pisses me off. I just found out that he was having an affair with her and I don't know if he would have told me or not'. The questions of where primary loyalty lay in his family, between adults, or between parent and children, was for him, as for many stressed children, a very important question. Over a number of sessions his pre-occupation that his father and mother would stay connected was talked out more openly and discussed as one of many forms of love. Earlier in the chapter I referred to 'nuanced meanings' of words. Here the family discuss what 'love' means.

Bob (10) his half sister Jane (15) and their mother, are discussing love.

| | |
|---|---|
| JANE: | Even though Dad and Mum did love each other very much it wasn't a working relationship. |
| BOB: | They loved each other too much. |
| JANE: | He and Mum couldn't live together, quite honestly, and Mum and Peter can live together. |
| BOB: | Yeah, they get on real well, they haven't had a single argument. Mum told me she loved Dad too much. |
| JANE: | I think loving someone too much means needing them too much. |
| MUM: | The emotions too much to actually deal with . . . you can't sort life out rationally, it becomes too emotional and passionate. You can't discuss shopping lists or paying the gas bill. |
| JANE/BOB (in synchrony): | Without it coming some sort of argument. |
| BOB: | I don't know if my Dad still loves my Mum. He's not in love with her but he still loves her like I love her. |
| JANE: | He does still love her, yes? |
| BOB: | I mean I'm not in love with my Mum. (To Mum): Do you still love him? |
| MUM: | Probably, yes, in a way. |

| | |
|---|---|
| BOB: | You're not in love with him, but you love him. |
| MUM: | In a way. |
| BOB: | Like she's not in love with me, but she loves me. |
| MUM (thoughtfully): | Yes. |
| BOB: | Or Granny, or Tabby (The cat)<br>(There follows a long discussion about Tabby, the cat, and loving him and how he had to be put down and how Bob had specially cared for him.) |
| | A post divorce dilemma that professionals may well be confronted with in relation to love includes helping children think about where they should live. Loyalty issues will be paramount here. |
| BOB (on choosing): | I was watching this programme 'Family Matters' and in the year 2000 there are going to be about two and a half million parents split up and the children could be told to choose, and then they could think . . . Oh I'll want my Mum and then they could think, Oh my Dad will think 'they don't love me' and then they could go to the Dad and the mother could think . . . and what I don't like is that they could go to the mother and then think maybe they should love their Dad more . . . or their mother. |

It may be useful to remember in the process of helping children think about where to live, that the pre-divorce pathways for boys and girls may well have had a gendered difference. Boys seem more likely to respond to marital conflict by becoming oppositional, whereas girls tend to become tearful. These behaviours will evoke different responses, the boys perhaps provoking further angry and punitive behaviour from already angry parents, whereas girls' tears provide an opportunity for a cuddle. This should not be interpreted as meaning that boys do not 'care'. As has already been touched on, the problems for boys can lie in knowing how care can be shown, since displays of emotional feeling from boys are often discouraged by adults.

## Children From Families Where Violence and Abuse are Part of the Family Pattern

Where children also have to learn to manage a form of parental or inter-parental violence, the question of what protects them or moderates the situation on their behalf is crucial. When professionals have to meet children from families where their safety is at risk issues of power and the silencing effect of coercive systems of behaviour on children's voices are particularly important to bear in mind. This may apply to boys as well as girls, but the incidence of reported violence shows that it is more likely to be an issue in relation to girls. Families where violence occurs are characterized by patriarchal views pervading the childhood of one or both parents; women and children are often accepted as appropriate victims of violence or abuse. Stresses in the current family can trigger the release of models learnt in the original family.

Since families where violence is part of the family modality have some features in common, understanding something of these may throw the difficulties of talking with children into relief. Firstly, in such families, the amount of time spent with each other is likely to exceed the amount of time spent interacting with others. Children may therefore have had less experience than their peers in meeting with and exchanging views with others. Secondly, the degree of intensity, commitment and involvement within family interactions is higher than outside the family. Families where abuse occurs show a disproportionate expression of negative or aversive behaviour towards each other in the face of what may be relatively neutral differences. Many interactions are inherently conflict structured with winners or losers. This experience can be re-enacted with professionals. Thirdly, there may be deficient social skills in managing any differences. As coercion is used to resolve conflicts, children are unlikely to have their own voice in a professional interview.

Talking with boys or girls from families characterized by violence involves working patiently with the small details of violent episodes so that the child as well as the professional (and hopefully where the child is to remain at home, the parents) can build up their own openly shared knowledge base of how episodes build up and where they might be stopped along the way.

Three things have to be taken into account in considering how effective working with a family where violence is the modality is likely to be. (a) Can the violence stop for long enough for the person or people who constitute the family to be safe, or do they know how to achieve safety? (b) Will the violence stop for long enough between sessions for any positive changes in ideas or feelings developed in the course of the session to be amplified? (c) How much has the modality of violence in the family become part of the modality within which the children experience and express themselves in a number of contexts, i.e. the violence is not only contained within the family but may be a core part of the child's experience of himself and therefore carried into other parts of his everyday life (Sroufe and Fleeson, 1988).

Albert, for example, had to think about how he could 'bring down' his father's escalating tempers which, once triggered off, seemed to have a life of their own. These had originated in the father's experience of being disciplined by his own father, and the violence had intensified in the protracted divorce negotiation. Disciplining of his son was never called 'hitting' but was known as 'giving him the hand'. Albert was passionately attached to his father but frightened of the hitting. He did not understand the cues that meant he was in for one of these attacks and his normal recourse had been to say he would tell his Mum. The first thing that seemed to be important in talking with him (as well as his father) was to break down the incident into details of what actually happened, then to link it to bodily feelings of hurt, upset, tears, and bruises and then having broken it down to think about specific ways of stopping it. Albert had learnt to fight back but this had intensified the violence. His subsequent idea was that he could just slide to the floor and show how small or helpless he was. In further work with him and his father this routine for stopping the escalations of violence was ritualized into an agreed code. Since Dad was devoted to his son, words to emphasize his smallness and his youth were used to break into father's stream of thought; 'small, little, child, too much'. The important gender move for both father and son was to move from a pattern of violent action and reaction to one where feelings of tenderness could be evoked and built on.

### Adolescence

Interviewing young people who have broken away from parental control carries its own hazards for the professional who is likely to re-arouse the same rage as the 'stupid' and uncomprehending parent. 'Like for fuck's sake what kind of an asshole do you think I am?', is a powerful rhetorical question but should not be answered with the same degree of hype, since it is more a request for a meeting point than an attempt to put the interviewer down. 'Who is the fucking nutter round here, you or me?', may suggest that the interviewer is on the wrong tack and should try a different one; and 'Sod off, I don't have to say nothing' suggests the young person is feeling despondent. In other words adolescents, when under stress, can show it powerfully whatever their gender.

As has been discussed above boys will be more likely to come in on an aggressive anti-social ticket than girls. Girls who do come to attention in this way may well bring complex issues with them (Caspi *et al.*, 1993; Cohen *et al.*, 1993; Cooklin, 1993: Maughan and Garratt, 1994).

Perhaps the most comprehensive piece of professional wisdom is to try and listen with respect whatever the story; not to get adversarial; not to allow yourself to feel put down or to take it personally; and not to try and impose another story on the narrative until it has been heard through since however angry the young person, they are still young and may be open to some other understandings if they feel listened to. I can only say that this gets easier with experience.

An important dimension of interviewing adolescents is acknowledging their accumulated life experience. This is unlikely to emerge in sequence but rather in fragments of the larger jigsaw puzzle, each bit of the whole being important to piece together to understand the problem in context. Deana, who had been running from home and hiding out for days without letting her parents know her whereabouts, had a story of sexual abuse from her elder brother as well as her own adoption as part of her worries. Her own mother had given birth to a child when she was in her early teens and Deana felt increasingly that she was 'just like her'. At an age when gender identity is forming through rebellion against, as well as identification with, a person of the same sex the professional needs to be sensitive to statements attributed to 'someone else'. For Deana to say about her biological mother, 'stupid slut, getting pregnant' but to attribute these sentiments to her adoptive mother, means that there is a tussle as to which aspect of womanliness she will take on. Careful listening without too much expressed opinion is essential with adolescents as the next sentence may show how their thoughts are going. 'I just think I must be so like my mother, right . . . like she sounds exactly like me; like she says exactly what she thinks, she flips all the time. Also she sounds really strong and like she knows what she wants to do with her own life'.

## Sexual Abuse

For many young women society is perceived as sending messages that encourage violence against them, and then sometimes denying that violence. It is very important that the professional does not fall into that trap. Girls who report rape, harassment or assault are more likely to be telling the truth than not, and deserve the respect of an attempt to hear them or to make time to hear them. There is a large literature on sexual abuse and only a few points, relating to talking, will be addressed here. It is also important to hold in mind that many adolescent boys have had sexually abusive experiences of different kinds, which may form part of their underlying stress.

First it is important to remember that many girls as well as women choose to dissociate from abusive experience and may not wish to report on it directly. Some children want to talk about the specific details of an event and within that context decide how much they feel safe to say. Other children may create concrete and valid imaginative enactments, expressing a distinction between themselves and what was done to their bodies. When Anna first told her story at six years old, certain features were often repeated. She had learnt how to dissociate herself from painful or frightening experience by turning herself into an automaton . . . saying that the person who was telling the story was inside a machine which could speak and all she had to do was press the button and get it to play. To demonstrate this she turned the wastepaper basket (metal) upside down, climbed onto it, pressed an imaginary button and began to speak in a high robotic voice, describing what had happened to her.

John, aged 9, could not talk about his abuse at all, but at his first interview was encouraged to draw the man who had attacked him and made him perform fellatio while he was 'playing out' just round the corner from his house. Drawing the man on the blackboard and getting him to colour in the jogging suit, and then the less neutral details like his hands and his face (although not his penis) allowed him to bring out his story bit by bit. Stasia, aged 14, wanted to report on sexual abuse by her brother over a period of years. In telling her story what helped her find words was being encouraged to describe for the first time all the details of the experience; where it had happened, the time of day, the clothes she was wearing. Professionals need to remember that there may not be a language in some families for 'hidden' parts of the body, and putting the story into words may involve the creation of a vocabulary. In Stasia's family her mother had no words for any of the 'women's parts' and told Stasia that her own mother had slapped her when she tried to ask what her own period was when she first 'came on'; assuming it was the result of 'doing something naughty with boys'.

### Traumatic Life Events

Coping with painful life events takes on a number of mental forms. Common ones include the re-playing and re-enactment of the event through flashbacks triggered by small reminders, dreams or nightmares. 'The mind is like a video recorder, and it runs, you know, just constantly running and every now and again you get images, and every image is . . . too painful . . . you have to block that part out' — (a young man remembering a violent childhood and the break up of the family. Gorell Barnes *et al.*, 1995). What we do know from many different studies (Rutter, 1987; Fonagy *et al.*, 1991; Garmezy and Masten, 1994) is that talking can make a difference to the future. At the risk of oversimplification I attach some action points which may be taken from the above stories:

1  Do not push the child to go faster than they want to. Pay attention to the style in which boys or girls are used to conversing in their families.
2  Do not direct them into answers to questions, but give them options from which they may choose.
3  Pick up any hint you are getting that you are being experienced as abusive and discuss it openly. Don't deny it, explore it.
4  Do not encourage the child to go further into an experience if they show they do not want to at that moment be led into an area of terror that they do not feel ready to manage. This applies equally to boys and girls, but boys may show more bravado.
5  Do not tell the child that you can't manage what you are hearing or that you are frightened in a way that stops them proceeding with their own discovery/journey.

In clinical work it is helpful to have an adult colleague at hand to discuss any new or unexpected experiences. In relation to gender issues, it is always valuable to consult with a colleague of the same gender as the child, where that gender is different from your own. Where the culture is also unknown to you, try and find a consultant of the same gender and culture as the child. This does not need to be a professional person, but someone who can inform you about nuances of which you may not be aware.

## Conclusion

In this chapter I have placed gender centrally in relation to culture. Whatever the context in which adult and child meet, sensitivity to cultural nuances will be a key factor to meaningful communication. All adults need to remember that they too have been children; that developmental differences are of key importance in the words that are chosen and the way in which topics are approached. Child sized language is vital.

Lastly remember that children enjoy playfulness. To be able to lighten a heavy mood is a gift. For adults this may mean being less fearful of not being correct, risking showing your own ignorance and clumsiness about the child's world, while finding a moment in which both can state some common element of absurdity. Where a child can sense the positive intention and humour of an adult, a leap is often made to a more open way forward.

## References

ANDERSEN, T. (1992) 'Relationship, language and preunderstanding in the reflecting process', *Australian and New Zealand Journal of Family Therapy*, **11**, 2, pp.87–91.

BAKER MILLER, J. (1986) *Towards a New Psychology of Women*, Harmondsworth, Penguin.

CASPI, A., LYNAM, D., MOFFIT, T.E. and SILVA, P.A. (1993) 'Unravelling girls' delinquency: biological, dispositional and contextual contributions to adolescent behaviour', *Developmental Psychology*, **29**, pp.19–30.

COHEN, P., COHEN, J., KASEN, S., VELEZ, C.N., HARTMARK, C., JOHNSON, J., ROJAS, M., BROOK, J. and STREUNING, E.L. (1993) 'An epidemiological study of disorders in late childhood and adolescence 1. Age and Gender specific prevalence', *Journal of Child Psychology and Psychiatry*, **34**, pp.851–67.

COOKLIN, A. (1993) 'Psychological changes in adolescence', in BROOK, C. (Ed) *The Practice of Medicine in Adolescence*, London, Edward Arnold.

COOKLIN, A., DAWSON, N. and MCHUGH, B. (1994) *Family Therapy Basics: A Distance Training Pack*, London, Marlborough Family Service.

CORBOZ-WARNERY, A., FIVAZ-DEPEURSINGE, E., GERTSCH BETTENS, C. and FAVEZ, N. (1993) 'Systemic analysis of triadic father mother baby interactions', *Infant Mental Health Journal*, **12**, 3, pp.260–72.

DOWLING, E. (1993) 'Are Family Therapists Listening to the young: A psychological perspective', *Journal of Family Therapy*, **15**, pp.403–11.

FAIRBAIRN, W. (1952) *Psychoanalytic Studies of the Personality*, London, Routledge and Kegan Paul.

FONAGY, P., STEELE, M., MORAN, G. and HIGGITT, A. (1991) 'The capacity for understanding mental states: The reflective self in parent and child and its significance for security of attachment', *Infant Mental Health Journal*, **12**, 3, p.201.

FONAGY, P., STEELE, M., STEELS, H., HIGGITT, A. and TARGET, M. (1993) 'The theory and practice of resilience', *Journal of Child Psychology and Psychiatry*, **35**, 2, pp.231–57.

GARMEZY, N. and MASTEN, A. (1994) 'Chronic adversities', in RUTTER, M., TAYLOR, E. and HERSOV, L. (Eds) *Child and Adolescent Psychiatry: Modern Approaches*, 3rd edn., Oxford, Blackwell Scientific Publications, pp.191–208.

GILLIGAN, L. (1982) *In a Different Voice: Psychological Theory and Women's Development*, London, Harvard University Press.

GORELL BARNES, G. (1995) (in press) 'The mind and the body: Therapeutic work with sexual abuse', in ANDOLFI, M. and DI NICHILO ANDOLFI, M. (Eds) (to be published in Italian as part of the proceedings of the Sorrento Conference).

GORELL BARNES, G. and HENESY, S. (1994) 'Re-claiming a female mind from the experience of sexual abuse', in BURCK, C. and SPEED, B. (Eds) *Gender, Power and Relationships*, Routledge, London.

GORELL BARNES, G., THOMPSON, P., DANIEL, G. and BURCHHANDT, N. (1995) (in preparation) *Growing up in Step-families: Life Story Interviews*, NCDS Cohort 1958, University of Essex, Department of Sociology and Institute of Family Therapy, London.

GORELL BARNES, G. (1994) 'The intersubjective mind', in YELLOLY, M. (Ed) *Learning and Teaching in Social Work: Towards Reflective Practice*, London, Jessica Kingsley.

HASTE, H. (1987) 'Growing into rules', in BRUNER, J. and HASTE, H. (Eds) *The Child's Construction of the World*, London, Methuen.

JONES, A.R. (1986) 'Writing the body: Toward an understanding of *l'Ecriture feminine*', in SHOWALTER, E. (Ed) *The New Feminist Criticism*, London, Virago.

LLOYD, B. (1987) 'Social representations of gender', in BRUNER, J. and HASTE, H. (Eds) *The Child's Construction of the World*, Methuen, London.

LYTTON, H. and ROMNEY, D. (1991) 'Parents' differential socialisation of boys and girls: A meta analysis', *Psychological Bulletin*, **109**, pp.267–96.

MACCOBY, E.E. (1986) 'Social groupings in childhood: Their relationship to prosocial and antisocial behaviour in boys and girls', in OLWEUS, D., BLOCK, J. and RADKE-YARROW, M. (Eds) *Development of prosocial and antisocial behaviour in boys and girls: Research, theories and issues*, New York, Academic Press.

MACCOBY, E.E. (1988) 'Gender as a social category', *Developmental Psychology*, **24**, pp.755–65.

MAIN, M., KAPLAN, N. and CASSIDY, J. (1985) 'Security in infancy and adulthood: A move to the level of representation', in BRETHERTON, I. and WATERS, E. (Eds) *Growing Points of Attachment Theory and Research*, Monographs of the Society for Research in Child Development, Serial no 209. vol. 50. nos 1–2.

MAUGHAN, B. and GARRATT, K. (1994) 'Conduct disorder: The gender gap', *ACPP Review and Newsletter*, **16**, 6, pp.277–83.

McANINCH, C.B., MARIOLIS, M.B., MILICH, R. and HARRIS, M.J. (1993) 'Impression formation in children: Influence of gender and expectancy', *Child Development*, **64**, pp.1492–1506.

MURRAY, L. (1992) 'Impact of post natal depression on infant development; A naturalistic study and treatment trial', Paper given at the Fourth World Conference, Infant Mental Health Chicago.

OCHS, E. and TAYLOR, C. (1992) 'Family narrative as political activity', *Discourse and Society*, **3**, pp.301–40.

QUINTON, D. and RUTTER, M. (1984) 'Parents with children in care: 1. current circumstances and parents; 2. intergenerational continuities', *Journal of Child Psychology and Psychiatry*, **25**, pp.211–31.

RADKE-YARROW, M., RICHARDS, J. and WILSON, W.E. (1988) 'Child development in a network of relationships', in HINDE, R.A. and STEVENSON-HINDE, J. (Eds) *Relationships Within Families: Mutual Influences*, Oxford, Oxford Scientific Publications.

RUTTER, M. (1987) 'Psychosocial resilience and protective mechanisms', in ROLF, S., MASTER, A., CICCHETTI, D., MUERCHTERLEIN, K. and WEINTRAUB, S. (Eds) *Risk and Protective Factors in the Development of Psychopathology*, New York, Cambridge University Press.

RUTTER, M. (1989) 'Intergenerational continuities and discontinuities in serious parenting difficulties', in CICCHETTI, D. and CARLSON, V. (Eds) *Child Maltreatment: Theory and Research on the Causes and Consequences of Child Abuse and Neglect*, Cambridge, Cambridge University Press.

SROUFE, A. and FLEESON, J. (1988) 'The coherence of family relationships', in HINDE, R.A. and STEVENSON-HINDE, J. (Eds) *Relationships within Families: Mutual Influence*, Oxford, Oxford Scientific Publications.

STEADMAN, C. (1985) 'Listen, how the caged bird sings: Amarjit's song', in STEADMAN, C., URWIN, C. and WALKERDINE, V. (Eds) *Language, Gender and Childhood*, London, Routledge and Kegan Paul.

STERN, D. (1977) *The First Relationship: Infant and Mother*, Fontana Open Books.

STERN, D. (1985) *The Interpersonal World of the Infant: A view from psychoanalysis and developmental psychology*, New York, Basic Books.

VYGOTSKY, L.S. (1981) 'The genesis of higher mental functions', in WERTSCH, J.V. (Ed) *The Concept of Activity in Soviet Psychology*, Armonk New York, M.E. Sharpe.

WHITE, M. and EPSTON, D. (1989) *Narrative Means to Therapeutic Ends*, New York, W.W. Norton & Co.

# 10   Race and the Child's Perspective

*Kedar N. Dwivedi*

In interacting with ethnic minority children and their families it is important to be aware of the significance of different aspects of the communication process which relate to ethnicity and cultural values and identity and also to have an appreciation of the interplay of these factors with those of racism and cultural conflict. In this chapter an attempt will be made to examine some of these aspects.

## Language

The importance of cultural differences in attitudes, values and beliefs in the use and development of language and, hence in communication, is not always appreciated by professionals yet an understanding of these differences is central to effective communication between adults and children, particularly where those adults and children come from different cultural or racial backgrounds. The limitations of children's linguistic abilities add to the difficulties of communicating between languages and different sets of images and metaphors mean that it is not easy to make sense of inner experiences and feelings without an appreciation of the conceptual differences which underlie ostensibly common experiences.

There are numerous examples of contrasting meaning of images and metaphors. Owls, for example, because of their big eyes, symbolize wisdom in western cultures but in Indian culture they symbolize the opposite because of their association with darkness. Similarly, the colour red in western cultures is often associated with anger but in the east it has a connotation of warmth and affection. During an Indian wedding, for example, one may find the entire scene flooded with red including the invitation cards. In western cultures, white or silver is usually associated with weddings but in the Indian culture white is seen as being more suitable for funeral ceremonies.

In relation to the expression of mental phenomena, feelings and relationships, there is also a tendency amongst mental health and other professionals to perceive ethnic minorities as less psychologically aware or to perceive their languages as less sophisticated. For example, many western psychiatrists perceive Asians as somatisers, that is, having a tendency to express emotional distress in terms of bodily symptoms. In fact, Asian languages are extremely rich in the variety of words for different shades of mental states and different aspects of mental phenomena and feelings. Indeed, there is a profuse use of idioms involving bodily sensations and functions which results from the integrated 'mind-body' approach in the eastern thinking, in contrast to the mind–body splitting and excessive psychologization of western approaches (Krause, 1993).

Similarly when it comes to describing relationships, the richness of eastern concepts are not easy to translate into English. The word 'cousin', illustrates this struggle extremely well. It is impossible to find an Indian equivalent for the word cousin. A child brought up in the extended family systems of the Indian subcontinent may call a male cousin, 'chachera bhai', if he is his paternal uncle's son; 'mamera bhai' if he is his maternal uncle's son; 'mausera bhai' if he is his mother's sister's son, 'fufera bhai' if he is his father's sister's son, and so on. Female cousins are similarly differentiated. Such a rich variety of terminology assists in defining the nature of the relationships including the etiquette and manners involved in relating to different types of cousins. The words 'uncle' and 'aunt' involve the same complexity. However, in the western context, a difficulty in using such words or concepts, can be easily misinterpreted as a sign of child's, or parent's, poor grasp of language or a sign of poverty of their language.

In listening to children, it is also important to keep in mind the fact that even at the individual level, language, attitude and personal identity are intimately related.

> Language is closely linked to an individual's sense of identity and hence to culturally transmitted values and modes of being. Language could be seen as the agent of transmission of cultural or 'ethnic' attributes in that it embodies, through its form and content, the communication patterns and object-relations which are intrinsic to the community from which it is derived. In families whose members speak more than one language there are important issues of tradition, identity and autonomy being expressed via the respective use of one or other language. Metaphorically, it could be said that language is to culture what DNA is to genetics. (Zulueta, 1990, p.264)

Further, it has been shown that bilingual individuals have different values and even gender roles, depending upon which language they use (Ervin, 1964). When bilinguals speak in their second language their lack of proficiency affects their perception of themselves in relation to others; they may feel that they themselves are less intelligent, happy or confident and this can block and distort their affective communication (Marcos and Urcuyo, 1979; Kline *et al.*, 1980).

## The Use of Interpreters

The fact that, for many ethnic minority families English is a second language, poses particular difficulties for effective communication. Not unnaturally, people can feel handicapped being interviewed in their second language and it is not easy to explore the nuances of people's intrapsychic and affective worlds when working in a second language. One way of dealing with this problem is by using an interpreter who is fluent in their first language but this is far from ideal. The children and their families have no way of knowing if they have been properly understood and, apart from the frustration which professionals can experience in conducting an interview through an interpreter, the professionals may equally feel unsure that their meaning has been accurately communicated and left out of certain discussions between the interpreter and the child or the family.

For the process to succeed requires a great deal of preparation beforehand so that during the interview an atmosphere is created whereby each party feels fully connected to the process. As this is difficult to achieve, many professionals end up resisting conducting interviews with the help of interpreters (Zulueta, 1984). This is exacerbated by the fact that many professionals do not have easy access to well prepared and competent interpreters. A recent survey conducted with members of ethnic minority populations regarding the Health Service, revealed that 65 per cent of patients who needed an interpreter were never offered one (Leisten and Richardson, 1994). Equally, many health authorities and hospitals still depend upon other professionals (on a voluntary basis) who happen to know another language but may not have time, energy or inclination to help adequately in this matter.

When an interpreter is available, the situation can be optimized by professionals making it clear that they value the role of the interpreter and orienting and preparing the interpreter for the interview (Mares *et al.*, 1985). It is important to introduce the interpreter to the family and to allow the interpreter to talk to the family and explain their background and so on, before they start interpreting. The interpreter may have to reassure the family of their trustworthiness and also remind the family to speak slowly and to allow time for translation. If the professional becomes impatient, the interpreter may begin to leave things out.

There is a tendency to use children from within families as interpreters. This has obvious disadvantages in terms of encouraging open communication not only because of the linguistic limitations of children but also because of the way in which this involves children in family issues which may be emotionally embarrassing, traumatic or draining and because of the effect it can have on family dynamics by changing the status of the child who is acting as the interpreter and by the alliance which he or she then has with the professional rather than the family.

### Body Language

In communication, it is not only the words used that matter but also the tone, gestures, facial expressions and other aspects of body language that have, in fact, an impact. The intonations of one's mother tongue are extremely hard to change and even when someone has mastered a new language old intonations tend to carry over and can sound abrupt, odd, irritating or even rude. Similarly, body language is also culturally conditioned. Words and gestures associated with politeness and good manners, for example, differ from culture to culture. In western cultures, eye contact is an important aspect of a conversation signalling honesty, attentiveness, respect, assertiveness, freedom from guilt, shame and so on. In eastern cultures, on the other hand, looking down is a way of showing respect and signals being well mannered. However, the poorly informed professionals may find this irritating and put pressure on the person to establish eye contact.

Different cultures have different traditions about meetings, greetings, saying farewell and expressing likes and dislikes. The western tradition of saying 'good morning', 'good bye' or shaking hands may not feel appropriate for some one who may feel more comfortable bowing or folding palms. Similarly 'please' and 'thank you' are nonverbally expressed in the east rather than spoken. In the east the emphasis is on action rather than words.

### Indirect Communication

For any professional to listen to ethnic minority children in order to discern and comprehend their true feelings, wishes and viewpoints requires sensitivity and openness to a variety of alternative communication styles and cultural perspectives. All professionals, social workers, family therapists, psychotherapists, teachers, solicitors and judges, are influenced by the cultural conditioning of their own social group. Though they may aspire to rise above these limits it is difficult for anyone to step outside their belief systems and to be open to a wide range of cultural possibilities because such differences and ambiguities can be threatening and lead to questioning of ones own methods of handling, coping with or treating life's issues. But, it has been argued that 'western' culture is characterized by a linear mode of thinking which makes it particularly difficult to assimilate the fact that other languages and cultures may encode a host of different cultural assumptions and interconnective, systemic perspectives (McGoldrick, 1982; Hodes, 1989; Zulueta, 1990).

An important aspect of child rearing practices in eastern cultures is training in becoming sensitive to other's feelings and also the training in dealing with one's own feelings. As young children mature and receive training in urinary and faecal continence, they are also expected to develop emotional continence and a capacity to gradually self regulate their affect (Dwivedi, 1993a). Unlike the western ideal of self-expression, eastern cultures aim to express feelings in ways that are not harmful either to oneself, or, to others. This, obviously, influences the style of communication placing more value on indirect and metaphorical communication than direct and clear communication as emphasized in western cultures. In fact, one of the most important aspects of training in many eastern religions is the better handling of feelings through expanding one's consciousness, getting in touch with one's emotions at the subtlest levels, accepting them, discerning their transitory nature and transmuting them by harnessing their energy to one's advantage, sometimes described metaphorically as 'tiger taming' (Rimpoche, 1987).

### Channels of Communication

Effective communication between professionals and children (and families) from ethnic minority backgrounds also requires an understanding of different attitudes towards the appropriateness or otherwise of particular types of communication. For example, to ask children in front of their parents to comment on their parents' behaviour could make them feel very uncomfortable. In cultures where open and direct expression of wishes and feelings are not encouraged, there are usually elaborate infrastructures for finding out, communicating and protecting the interests of various parts of the extended family system. Thus, in families from eastern cultures, the children may not openly express their objections or wishes to their parents although other members of the extended family, such as grandparents, uncles and aunts and certain siblings who also have a very strong bond with the child, can have direct access to their feelings and opinions. These members of the extended family or the key relatives then act as intermediaries to ensure that parents are either aware of the children's feelings or are acting in children's best interest. Some relatives, such as the grandparents, may be constantly attuned to the needs of the little ones and may also have the power to directly intervene on their behalf and influence parental decisions. These 'intermediaries' thus have an important protective role in the family, but their success or failure depends upon their skill in the way they conduct these protective functions.

The delicacy of these roles, although hard to fully appreciate, must be comprehended by the professional for communication to be really effective. Furthermore, professionals can play an important role in discovering and establishing channels of communication. As most of the ethnic minority families who have migrated to this country represent only part of a larger family structure, they do not have the same extended family systems as they would have had in their country of origin. Thus, the intermediary infrastructure may have been lost, disintegrated or disqualified in a different cultural climate or may exist in a rudimentary or modified forms. An attempt by a professional to explore, utilize and even assist in its repair can help establish contact with the different parts of the system including the feelings, wishes and opinions of the child.

Having a professional qualification, status or experience may not be enough to establish such links as different cultures have different images of the helping professions. In the author's experience the most relevant credentials of a professional in establishing such links are likely to be not so much the qualification, salary and the status of the professional, but their respect for moral values and their conduct, a glimpse of which can only be obtained in an informal relationship.

Thus, investing time, effort, and energy in getting to know a child or a family, allowing opportunities for the enactment and unfolding of curiosity, respect and values in action and not just in words, can be extremely helpful in opening up essential channels of communication.

## Professional Inhibitions, Clumsiness and Oversensitivity

It is impossible for any professional to be fully knowledgeable of the cultural contexts of all children. It should, however, be possible to develop and maintain a curious and respectful frame of mind in listening to children and their families which implies a respect for the differences which will inevitably exist in cultural attitudes and values. It should also be possible for all professionals to be open to learning from children and their families about those differences. Such a process may at times be clumsy both on the part of the professional and of the family members but an atmosphere, where the inevitableness of clumsiness is openly acknowledged, can be conducive to mutual education. Otherwise, fear of clumsiness can lead to inhibitions and mistaken assumptions, the actions arising from which may be disastrous. Storti (1989), for example, demonstrates how fear or anger can easily arise when we find others to be different from what we expected and how this can prompt us to withdraw from meaningful communication. What begins innocently as reflexive self protection can quickly lead to rejection of the other culture and feeling uncomfortable among people from that culture.

It is not only the differences in various aspects of language and communication but also the cultural differences which exist within our society in relation to basic concepts such as 'dependability' and 'independence', the value of the family and the expectations for behaviour that follow from these which are so important if any professional is genuine in wanting to understand better what children have to say. Fundamental differences in the context of cultural racism on the one hand, and the experiences of overt or direct racial discrimination and abuse on the other, further compound the situation.

## Race and Ethnicity

'Race' is not an objective category although the process of categorization on racial lines does continue. It is in fact, a social construction in which the variations within the group said to be a 'race' are perceptually diminished, while the variations between groups are perceptually emphasized, in spite of the fact that the phenotypical variations are continuous and not discrete (Thomas and Sillen, 1979). Smith (1986) pointed out that 'Race is an essentially biological concept based on those distinctive sets of hereditary phenotypical features that distinguish varieties of mankind' (p.189), but the facts are that

(a)   no race possesses a discrete package of genetic characteristics (Cooper, 1984)

(b)   there is more genetic variation within than between races, and the genes responsible for morphological features such as skin colour (which are the basis of racial groupings) are very few and atypical (Hill, 1989).

Indeed, there is now a tendency to use the notion of 'ethnicity' more than that of race. Ethnicity is derived from a Greek word meaning people or tribe but here too the concept is neither simple nor precise. It can imply one or more of the following:

(a)   shared social background or origin,
(b)   shared language,
(c)   common culture and tradition, or
(d)   shared religion.

Ethnic boundaries are very imprecise and fluid and often confused with nationality or with migrant status (Bhopal *et al.*, 1991). The complexity of this is illustrated by Senior and Bhopal (1994) when they point out that:

immigrants from the Indian subcontinent to the United Kingdom may be British nationals but be members of a particular ethnic group such as Sikh Punjabis. Their children born in the United Kingdom are members of their parents' ethnic group but may perceive themselves part of a larger ethnic group such as Indian, Asian, or black. They may also perceive themselves to have an additional ethnic identity relating to the host community (such as British, Scottish, or Irish). Ethnicity, particularly self defined ethnicity, depends on the context in which the definition is made. (Senior and Bhopal, 1994, p.327)

Other terms in current use do little to clarify the situation. Further difficulties, for example, arise from the use of the words 'colour' and 'coloured'.

Colour was used as the primary visible signifier to distinguish 'us' from 'them'. In order to do this successfully it was necessary for the hallucinatory whitening of all the peoples of Europe including the Roman, the Greek, the Celt, and of course Jesus Christ, so that they could be distinguished from the 'coloured'. (Dalal, 1993, p.278)

In addition, the word 'ethnic' is often abused by referring to coloured populations or coloured families as 'ethnic populations' or 'ethnic families', as if others do not have any ethnicity! The Commission for Racial Equality, therefore, uses the term 'ethnic minorities', believing that cultural and religious differences are important. The Kings Fund, on the other hand, classes all disadvantaged groups as 'black' believing that the experience of racism is most important (McKenzie and Crowcroft, 1994).

Some use the term 'Afro-Caribbean' for people who are black and of Caribbean ancestry while others use it for people of African or Caribbean descent or for people from the West Indies who are of African origin. In fact, the population of the West Indies includes many different ethnic groups, and people of Indian origin are the most numerous; the use of the concept in this country presumably reflects the fact that immigrants from the West Indies have mainly been of African origin (Black, 1989).

## Ethnicity and Cultural Values

Ethnicity is transmitted essentially through the family and is also deeply tied to the family (McGoldrick, 1982). It patterns our way of thinking, feeling and behaving. Language is one of the factors that elaborates ethnicity and people from different ethnic groups may experience and express their distress differently (Patel, 1994).

As it is constantly changing, 'culture' is difficult to measure. It is also a difficult concept to define but can be usefully seen as a social construct comprising of the behaviours and attitudes of a social group including their beliefs, knowledge, morals, traditions and customs. It is determined by upbringing and choice (Fernando, 1991). Sometimes there is an emphasis on 'system of rules' governing behaviour but elsewhere on 'system of beliefs' while applying the notion of culture (McGoldrick *et al.*, 1982). Bateson (1958) regards cultures as symbolic systems constructed by the scientist while Geertz (1973) conceptualizes them as webs of meaning. Thus, culture organizes cognitive and emotional elements within families, patterning our thinking, feeling and behaviour in both subtle and obvious ways, though the cultural values and assumptions themselves may remain outside our awareness.

Child rearing practices are the most important manifestations of cultural assumptions and the cultural factors in upbringing have been shown to have an enormous impact on the development of the personality. They may reinforce or suppress certain specific internal conflicts, stimulate or suppress the use of certain types of defence mechanisms, thus making the expression of certain behaviours culture-specific (Erikson, 1965; Kakar, 1978; Andreou, 1992; Dwivedi, 1996a).

In the Eastern culture a person is seen as a part of the embedded inter-connectedness of relationships whereas in the Western culture there is an emphasis on separateness, clear boundaries, individuality and autonomy within the relationships. 'In Western cultures, individuality is the prime value and relatedness is secondary in the sense that a person has the choice of whether to make certain relationships with other entities or not' (Tamura and Lau, 1992, p.330). In eastern cultures there is a tendency not to separate or distinguish the individual from the social context, which is described by Shweder and Bourne (1982) in terms of 'sociocentric' conception of relationships in contrast to the 'egocentric' conceptions in western cultures.

Roland (1980) highlights differences as regards early child rearing practices between Western and Indian cultures. Accordingly in the Indian cultures, more emphasis is placed on 'dependability'. The parents are usually at pains to ensure that their children grow up in an atmosphere of indulgence, physical closeness, common sleeping arrangements, immediate gratification of physical and emotional needs and a prolonged babyhood. The young ones are there to be loved just for 'being' there rather than 'doing' the right things. The parents aim to become a model of dependability so that their children also grow up to become dependable.

Similarly DeVos, describing child rearing practices in Japan, writes:

Mothers tend to 'suffer' their children rather than to forbid or inhibit their behaviour by using verbal chastisement or even physical punishment. The child, while this form of discipline is going on, learns gradually the vulnerability of the loved one and that control of an offender is exercised not by doing any thing to the offender but by self-control. (DeVos, 1985, p.155)

Another manifestation of cultural embedding of interconnectedness of relationships is the value placed upon extended family life. For example, in India most people spend the formative years of their early childhood in an extended family setting because the cultural ideal of mastering narcissism can be best achieved through growing up in an extended family system. Moreover, it is impossible for an extended family system to be sustained without proactive training in mastering narcissism through extended family life. The biggest danger to an extended family is the possibility of its fracturing along the boundaries around nuclear units because the natural tendency of love is to be concentrated towards one's own. Therefore, an extra effort is required to redirect it across the nuclear family boundaries.

Perelberg (1992) has explored the links between culture and the patterns of interactions in families with the help of the concept of the 'family map'. The family map 'is the set of ideas which guide behaviour and emotions in everyday life, organise and systemise the world and transform it's sensory dimensions into intelligible ones' (Perelberg, 1992, p.117). The concept is particularly helpful in understanding the conflicting ideas and expectations which can be held by different members of a family, especially those of different generations. She describes two models of non-pathological maps as 'hierarchical' (segregated) and 'symmetrical' (egalitarian). Hierarchical or segregated role relationships refer to tasks and activities with the sociocentric view of individual in a role relationship. At the other end of the continuum is the 'Undifferentiated' (symmetrical, egalitarian, and 'democratic') family map which emphasises the autonomy of the individual.

## Social Dislocation

For many ethnic minority families, the impact of dislocation, loss of the extended family and other important social networks and the undermining of their value systems by the major institutions and local sub-cultures, can produce serious consequences. One recent survey in London has revealed an alarmingly high rate of emotional distress within South Asian communities and little outlet for expressing this distress (Beliappa, 1991). Another study in Tower Hamlets has shown that the Bangladeshi respondents were experiencing more serious life-events and reported more symptoms of psychological disturbance than their indigenous neighbours (MacCarthy and Craissati, 1989).

As many Asian parents:

> had a rather different upbringing which instilled rigorous moral standards, they begin to feel apprehensive about the possibility of their children not persevering with these traditional moral values. When the children's presentation, manners, attitudes, thoughts, and ideas diverge markedly from traditional patterns and from what the parents perceive as culturally appropriate and correct, they may fear the loss of their close links with their children. (Dwivedi, 1996, in press)

When the parents are also confronted by images of violence, drugs and overt sexuality in Western media they fear for the safety and well-being of their children and may respond with protective gestures of panic. Parental protectiveness, in turn, can escalate as the youngsters attempt to resist it. Many youngsters can find the pull in the opposite directions as rather distressing (Ahmed, 1986; Dwivedi, 1993b). Goldberg and Hodes (1992) describe how racism distorts the process of negotiation between ethnic minority parents and their adolescent children. Attempted suicide, for example, is more common amongst young Asian women than amongst the non-Asian British (Glover *et al.*, 1989; Merrill and Owens, 1986, 1988). This symbolizes the acting out of the 'poisonous view' of the dominant group regarding the minority cultures (Goldberg and Hodes, 1992).

## Cultural Conflicts and Racism

In addition to developing an awareness of the extent to which one's own cultural values may influence interactions with children and young people and their families, it is important also for professionals to be aware of the impact of cultural differences on the individual. These differences in cultural emphases can have great significance for understanding children's relationships with their families.

For example, in contrast to 'dependability' in the eastern culture, as mentioned above, 'autonomy' or independence of the individual is viewed as a cherished ideal in most western cultures. 'Western' parents are often at pains to make their children independent as soon as possible. Similarly, 'western' professionals, such as teachers, social workers, health professionals and counsellors, working with children, families or other individuals aim at fostering independence. Psychotherapists, group analysts and family therapists too consider individuation, autonomy and independence as fundamental aims of therapy. Children, therefore, are expected to have their own voices separate, different and even opposite to those of their parents or other relatives. In these contexts it can be considered appropriate for children and young people from other cultural and ethnic backgrounds to rebel against their own cultural expectations and to pursue more independent life styles than are acceptable within their families. If a child or adolescent doesn't express such an independent (or rebellious) view or behaviour, the assumption may be that the family organization is repressive and over-restrictive. Many professionals, therefore, feel passionate about rescuing, for example, Asian children and youngsters from their 'oppressive' and 'primitive' family values.

> Communication within the family is not on an equal footing as the adults around the youngster assume that they know what is best for him. If he does not feel separate from his parents in school, there is no way he could discover for himself what kind of life style he would want to adopt when he leaves his parents. Wanting to identify with western values and life style is a stage that many young Asians experience quite strongly — some will, for instance adopt English names and dress. (Personal communication from a school counsellor)

Similarly, a Deputy Headmistress of a school comments:

> We teach the girls to be independent and critical thinkers, but at home, they are taught the virtues of collective responsibility and unquestioning respect to the elders in the family'. (quoted in Ghuman, 1991, p.121)

Such ideological impositions are clearly a kind of cultural imperialism and a form of institutional racism, and in fact, against the spirit of the 1989 Children Act which recommends giving full consideration to the racial origin and ethnic, cultural, religious and linguistic background of the child.

The attitudes illustrated above help to maintain subconscious assumptions about the superiority of westernised family maps and child rearing practices and denigration of others (Ahmed, 1986). Asian families, for example, are criticized as being too self-contained, constricting and not being prepared to adjust to the British way of life (Littlewood and Lipsedge, 1989). The situation is mirrored in the novelist Ruth Prawer Jhabvala's observations:

> To live in India and be at peace, one must to a very considerable extent become Indian and adopt Indian attitudes, habits, beliefs, assume, if possible, an Indian personality. But how is this possible? And even if it

were possible — without cheating oneself would it be desirable? Should one try to become something other than what one is? (Jhabvala, 1987, p.21)

Hazlitt wrote about one of the common natural tendencies, 'The first thing an Englishman does on going abroad is to find fault with what is French, because it is not English' (quoted in Storti, 1989, p.47). 'Racism' refers to practices of racial discrimination, whether deliberate or unintentional and to beliefs based on racial prejudice. Prejudice literally means 'prejudging'. A person who holds views about an individual, or group of people, which are not based on knowledge, and is unwilling to change these views even when presented with clear evidence that they are factually wrong, is a prejudiced person. Institutional racism is the way in which the society's institutions operate to the continued advantage of the majority either intentionally or unintentionally. Racism both at the personal level in professionals and at the institutional level has been responsible for unnecessary reception into care of black children (Cheetham, 1982).

Many children experience stress in relation to school work, peer and social relationships, financial and social situations, dislocation, losses, separation, other stressful life events. Ethnic minority children, in addition to the above, are also often exposed to racism in the form of racial disadvantage, discrimination, prejudice, abuse and stresses arising from the undermining of their value systems. The Commission for Racial Equality (1988) and Troyna and Hatcher (1992) have described problems of racism and racial harassment and bullying in schools. Unfortunately, the tendency on the part of many people is to deny, disbelieve, ignore or even encourage such racial abuse, which leaves the people involved, especially if they are children, feeling helpless and hopeless (Beliappa, 1991; Dwivedi, 1996b, 1996c).

The fragmentation and loss of extended network support which many ethnic minority families experience along with the exposure to racist attitudes can often lead to children splitting-off aspects of themselves and projecting them onto others (Dwivedi, 1993c). For example, Rashida, a girl of Pakistani origin (Dwivedi, 1993d), during her early adolescence, had to go with her mother into a women's refuge because of the violent outbursts of her mentally ill father and the lack of other adequate support. The racially derogatory attitude of the other women in the refuge and of the children and teachers in her school led Rashida to develop strong negative feelings towards her ethnic origins. Being dislocated from her community into the refuge, Rashida's mother felt not only extremely distressed but also ashamed, which further fuelled Rashida's attitudes and the relationship between the two deteriorated to the extent that Rashida developed blind hatred towards the people of her ethnic origins, including her parents. In order to defend against the damaged self concept, she stripped off her 'bad' aspects into others and began to assert that her parents were not her real parents, that she must have been adopted by them and that at least one of her natural parents must have been white.

Sometimes the damage to self identity is so deep that a great deal of more help is required than just placing a child in an ethnically-appropriate (which too is seldom achieved) foster or other residential placement.

> Often social workers will have put thought and time into trying to make available black adults as foster parents or residential social workers to enable the children to identify with and relate to adults from their own race and cultural group. Their hope is that through these new relationships the children would begin to heal some of their own wounds and confusion about themselves. It is difficult for these workers to face the fact that this is often not enough, or worse, that such model figures can be rejected. Sometimes the emotions aroused by these children in the social workers are unbearable, making them feel desperate and useless. The children's and adolescents' expression of anger and rejection have an additional dimension: unlike white children in care, they also reject their own culture and race or identify negatively with it, at times experiencing disgust at the colour of their skins (Andreou, 1992, pp.146–7).

### Culturalistic Pseudo Insight

While it is important to recognize the importance of cultural differences, it is equally important to recognize the importance of individual differences in personality. Devereux (1953) has coined the term 'culturalistic pseudo insight' to describe the phenomenon of attributing to culture what is actually due to the individual personality differences. Ahmed (1985) also highlights this tendency in the professionals to place an uncritical reliance on cultural theories and culturally based explanations of the behaviour of ethnic minority families, behaviours which may in fact, arise from their individual and social circumstances. For example, restrictive, anxious, overprotective, neglectful, addictive, or violent behaviours may arise in any family from stress and dislocation, family disruption, breakdown of supportive social network, but when it comes to dealing with such behaviours in ethnic minority families, there is a tendency in the professionals to see it in terms of cultural factors. In fact this may even encourage certain family members accused of damaging behaviours to hide behind such cultural or religious explanations.

Similarly Fernando (1988) has highlighted the less obvious fact of the failure by social services and mental health agencies to provide good enough services to ethnic minority families

> . . . on the grounds that the (white) professional staff can not understand their cultural ways and that intervention is culturally inappropriate. Thus, sometimes, child neglect by black parents is overlooked and excused and families are allowed to suffer on the basis that they are being allowed to live according to their 'culture'. The result is a racist service based on expediency with 'culture' as an excuse. (Fernando, 1988, pp.166–7)

## Conclusion

When working with children and families from minority ethnic backgrounds it is important to help and support them in ways that enhance and do not damage their self identity, particularly those of the children. The Children Act emphasizes the value of ethnic, linguistic and cultural sensitivity in service provisions. In addition to the issues of language differences there are also important cultural differences in style of communication. For example, as was noted above, in contrast to the emphasis placed on clear and direct communication in the western culture, there is an emphasis on indirect and metaphorical communication in eastern cultures. Similarly, as noted above also there are cultural differences in the values placed on individuality. In the western culture independence, autonomy and individuation are seen as the cherished ideal while interconnectedness, dependability and transcending narcissism are the cherished ideals in the eastern culture.

In practice there is an enormous potential for improvement. For example, the Commission for Racial Equality (1992) launched the Race Relations Code of Practice in Primary Health Care Services with the aim of facilitating fair access in the provision of services. The code was drawn up in consultation with General Practitioners, Family Health Service Authorities (FHSAs), Community Health Councils, Regional and District Health Authorities and a wide range of other related health bodies. However, when the FHSAs were contacted by the CRE in 1993 only 29 out of 600 contacted indicated that they were planning to implement the code.

There is also a tendency in the professionals to deny, disbelieve or ignore, racist attitudes, racial harassment and bullying that a large number of children and their families experience. According to the Commission for Racial Equality (Chan, 1995) 130,000 racial attacks occur in this country annually and the black and ethnic minority people are twice as likely to be unemployed compared with white people. The media, particularly the popular press are usually biased in the way they report racial incidents and issues.

Further, as Dayal (1990) points out, the emotional availability of many professionals to ethnic minorities is often very limited either due to personal or institutional racism or due to the fear of clumsiness and its consequences. Some fail to engage on the grounds that they can not understand the cultural ways of ethnic minority families (Fernando, 1988) while others look for and quickly find 'cultural conflict' arguments to support their position. There is also a tendency for professionals (and families) to dress up individual issues as cultural or religious matters. For a professional, therefore, to think that abuse may be culturally acceptable by a certain community, is failing as an agent of protection, with an excuse of being oversensitive.

## References

AHMED, S. (1985) 'Cultural racism in work with women and girls', in FERNANDO, S. (Ed) *Women: Cultural Perspectives*, Report of Conference organized by the Transcultural Psychiatry Society (UK), London, TCPS (UK).

AHMED, S. (1986) 'Cultural racism in work with Asian women and girls', in AHMED, S., CHEETHAM, J. and SMALL, J. (Eds) *Social Work with Black Children and their Families*, London, Batsford.

ANDREOU, C. (1992) 'Inner and outer reality in children and Adolescents', in KAREEM, J. and LITTLEWOOD, R. (Eds) *Intercultural Therapy*, Oxford, Blackwell Scientific Publications.

BATESON, G. (1958) *Naven*, Stanford, Stanford University Press.

BELIAPPA, J. (1991) *Illness or Distress: Alternative Models of Mental Health*, London, Confederation of Indian Organisations.

BHOPAL, R.S., PHILLIMORE, P. and KOHLI, H.S. (1991) 'Inappropriate use of the term Asian: An obstacle to ethnicity and health research', *Journal of Public Health Medicine*, **13**, pp.244–46.

BLACK, J. (1989) *Child Health in a Multi-cultural Society*, London, British Medical Journal.

CHAN, M. (1995) *Personal Communication*.

CHEETHAM, J. (Ed) (1982) *Social Work and Ethnicity*, London, Allen and Unwin.

COMMISSION FOR RACIAL EQUALITY (1988) *Learning in Terror: A Survey of Racial Harassment in Schools and Colleges*, London, CRE.

COMMISSION FOR RACIAL EQUALITY (1992) *Race Relations Code of Practice in Primary Health Care Services*, London, CRE.

COOPER, R. (1984) 'A note on the biological concept of race and its application in epidemiological research', *American Heart Journal*, **108**, pp.715–23.

DALAL, F.N. (1993) 'Race and Racism: An attempt to organise difference', *Group Analysis*, **26**, pp.277–93.

DAYAL, N. (1990) 'Psychotherapy services for minority ethnic communities in the NHS — a psychotherapist's view', *Midland Journal of Psychotherapy*, **11**, pp.28–37.

DEVEREUX, G. (1953) 'Cultural factors in psycho-analytic theory', *Journal of American Psycho-analytic Association*, **1**, pp.629–55.

DEVOS, G.A. (1985) 'Dimensions of the self in Japanese culture', in MARSELLA, A.J., DEVOS, G.A. and HSU, F.L.K. (Eds) *Culture and Self: Asian and Western Perspectives*, London, Tavistock Publications.

DWIVEDI, K.N. (1993a) 'Emotional development', in DWIVEDI, K.N. (Ed) *Groupwork with Children and Adolescents: A Handbook*, London, Jessica Kingsley.

DWIVEDI, K.N. (1993b) 'Confusion and underfunctioning in children', in VARMA, V.P. (Ed) *How and Why Children Fail*, London, Jessica Kingsley.

DWIVEDI, K.N. (1993c) 'Child abuse and hatred', in VARMA, V.P. (Ed) *How and Why Children Hate*, London, Jessica Kingsley.

DWIVEDI, K.N. (1993d) 'Coping with unhappy children who are from ethnic minorities', in VARMA, V.P. (Ed) *Coping with Unhappy Children*, London, Cassell.

DWIVEDI, K.N. (1996a) 'Culture and personality', in DWIVEDI, K.N. and VARMA, V.P. (Eds) *Meeting the Needs of Ethnic Minority Children: A Handbook for Professionals*, London, Jessica Kingsley (in press).

DWIVEDI, K.N. (1996b) 'Stress in children from ethnic minorities', in VARMA, V.P. (Ed) *Coping with Stress in Children*, Aldershot, Arena (in press).

DWIVEDI, K.N. (1996c) 'Introduction', in DWIVEDI, K.N. and VARMA, V.P. (Eds) *Meeting the Needs of Ethnic Minority Children: A Handbook for Professionals*, London, Jessica Kingsley (in press).

DWIVEDI, R. (1996) 'Community and Youthwork with Asian Women and Girls', in DWIVEDI, K.N. and VARMA, V.P. (Eds) *Meeting the Needs of Ethnic Minority Children: A Handbook for Professionals*, London, Jessica Kingsley (in press).

ERIKSON, E. (1965) *Childhood and Society*, Harmondsworth, Penguin.

ERVIN, S.H. (1964) 'Language and TAT content in bilinguals', *Journal of Abnormal Psychology*, **68**, pp.500–7.

FERNANDO, S. (1988) *Race and culture in psychiatry*, London, Croom Helm.

FERNANDO, S. (1991) *Mental health, race and culture*, London, Macmillan.

GEERTZ, C. (1973) *The Interpretation of Cultures*, New York, Basic Books.

GHUMAN, P.A.S. (1991) 'Best or worst of two worlds? A study of Asian adolescents', *Educational Research*, **33**, pp.121–32.

GLOVER, G., MARKES, F. and NOWERS, M. (1989) 'Parasuicide in young Asian women', *British Journal of Psychiatry*, **154**, 7, pp.271–2.

GOLDBERG, D. and HODES, M. (1992) 'The poison of racism and the self poisoning of adolescents', *Journal of Family Therapy*, **14**, pp.51–67.

HILL, A.V.S. (1989) 'Molecular markers of ethnic groups', in CRUICKSHANK, J.K. and BEEVERS, D.G. (Eds) *Ethnic Factors in Health and Disease*, London, Wright.

HODES, M. (1989) 'Annotation: Culture and family therapy', *Journal of Family Therapy*, **11**, pp.117–28.

JHABVALA, R.P. (1987) *Out of India*, New York, Simon and Schuster.

KAKAR, S. (1978) *The Inner World: A Psychoanalytic Study of Childhood and Society in India*, New York and Delhi, Oxford University Press.

KLINE, F., ACOSTA, F.X., AUSTIN, W. and JOHNSON, R.G. (1980) 'The misunderstood Spanish-speaking patient', *American Journal of Psychiatry*, **137**, pp.1530–3.

KRAUSE, I.-B. (1993) 'Family therapy and anthropology: A case for emotions', *Journal of Family Therapy*, **15**, pp.35–56.

LEISTEN, R. and RICHARDSON, J. (1994) *Access to Health: A Minority Ethnic Perspective*, Nothampton, Nene College.

LITTLEWOOD, R. and LIPSEDGE, M. (1989) *Aliens and Alienists: Ethnic Minorities and Psychiatry*, London, Unwin Hyman.

MARCOS, L.R. and URCUYO, L. (1979) 'Dynamic psychotherapy with the bilingual patient', *American Journal of Psychotherapy*, **33**, pp.331–8.

MACCARTHY, B. and CRAISSATI, J. (1989) 'Ethnic differences in response to adversity: A community sample of Bangladesh and their indigenous neighbours', *Journal of Social Psychiatry and Psychiatric Epidemiology*, **24**, pp.196–201.

MARES, P., HENLEY, A. and BAXTER, C. (1985) *Health Care in Multi-cultural Britain*, Cambridge, Health Education Council and National Extension College.

McGOLDRICK, M. (1982) 'Ethnicity and family therapy', in McGOLDRICK, M., PEARCE, J.K. and GIARDANO, J. (Eds) *Ethnicity and Family Therapy*, New York/London, Guilford Press.

McGOLDRICK, M., PEARCE, J. and GIARDANO, J. (Eds) (1982) *Ethnicity and Family Therapy*, New York, Guilford Press.

McKENZIE, K.J. and CROWCROFT, N.S. (1994) 'Race, ethnicity, culture and science: Researchers should understand and justify their use of ethnic groupings', *British Medical Journal*, **309**, pp.286–7.

MERRILL, J. and OWENS, J. (1986) 'Ethnic differences in selfpoisoning: A comparative study of Asian and white groups', *British Journal of Psychiatry*, **148**, pp.708–12.

MERRILL, J. and OWENS, J. (1988) 'Self-poisoning among immigrant groups', *Acta Psychiatrica Scandinavica*, **77**, pp.77–80.

PATEL, V. (1994) 'The cross-cultural assessment of depression', *Focus on Depression*, **2**, 1, pp.5–8.

PERELBERG, R.J. (1992) 'Familiar and unfamiliar types of family structure: Towards a conceptual framework', in KAREEM, J. and LITTLEWOOD, R. (Eds) *Intercultural Therapy: Themes, Interpretations and Practices*, Oxford, Blackwell Scientific Publications.

RIMPOCHE, D.A. (1987) *Taming the Tiger*, Eskdalemuir, Dzalendra Publishing.

ROLAND, A. (1980) 'Psychoanalytic perspectives on personality development in India', *International Review of Psychoanalysis*, **1**, pp.73–87.

SENIOR, P.A. and BHOPAL, R. (1994) 'Ethnicity as a variable in epidemiological research', *British Medical Journal*, **309**, pp.327–30.

SHWEDER, R.A. and BOURNE, E.J. (1982) 'Does the concept of the person vary cross-culturally?', in MARSELLA, A.J. and WHITE, G.M. (Eds) *Cultural Conceptions of Mental Health and Therapy*, Dordrecht, D. Reidel Publishing Company.

SMITH, M.G. (1986) 'Pluralism, race and ethnicity in selected African countries', in REX, J. and MASON, D. (Eds) *Theories of Race and Ethnic Relations*, Cambridge, Cambridge University Press.

STORTI, C. (1989) *The Act of Crossing Cultures*, Intercultural Press.

TAMURA, T. and LAU, A. (1992) 'Connectedness versus separations: Applicability of family therapy to Japanese families', *Family Process*, **31**, 4, pp.319–40.

THOMAS, A. and SILLEN, S. (1979) *Racism and Psychiatry*, New York, Citadel Press.

TROYNA, B. and HATCHER, R. (1992) *Racism in Children's Lives: A Study of Mainly White Schools*, London, Routledge and National Children's Bureau.

ZULUETA, F. De (1984) 'Bilingualism: A review', *Psychological Medicine*, **14**, pp.541–57.

ZULUETA, F. De (1990) 'Bilingualism and family therapy', *Journal of Family Therapy*, **12**, pp.255–65.

# Notes on Contributors

**Dr Ron Davie** is a free-lance consultant psychologist, and trainer in the special needs field. He also carries out assessments as an expert witness on children's cases, largely in the High Court. He was the first elected President of the National Association for Special Educational Needs and is a former Director of the National Children's Bureau.

**Dr Kedar Nath Dwivedi** is a consultant in child and adolescent Psychiatry at Northampton and a clinical teacher in the Faculty of Medicine at the University of Leicester. He graduated in medicine from the Institute of Medical Sciences, Varanasi, India and served as an Assistant Professor in Preventive and Social Medicine in Simla before moving to the UK in 1974. He has written widely on many aspects of child and adolescent psychiatry and meeting the needs of ethnic minority children.

**Dr Irvine Gersch** is principal educational psychologist for the London Borough of Waltham Forest and has worked as a teacher and Open University tutor. He is a chartered psychologist and is currently Chair of the British Psychological Society's Training Committee for educational psychologists. He has published widely in the area of pupil involvement, behaviour management, school change and management.

**Dr Danya Glaser** is a consultant child and adolescent psychiatrist and family therapist. She is currently working in Great Ormond Street Hospital for Children, having previously worked at Guy's Hospital. She has a special interest in child abuse and protection, and has written, taught and carried out research in this field. The rights of children are of central concern to her practice.

**Gill Gorell Barnes** has worked with children in different mental health contexts since 1966. She began work in the Children's Department of Islington Social Services and worked at the Maudsley Hospital before joining the Child and Family Services in Hackney. She currently practices and teaches at the Tavistock Clinic and is involved in research with children in step families and in families going through divorce and post-divorce transitions. She has a special interest in adoption.

**Neil Hall** is consultant psychologist at TEAM Health Care, Knowle and Honorary Lecturer in the School of Education, The University of Birmingham. He regularly provides expert testimony on behalf of children and their families in court proceedings and publishes and teaches on matters relating to child protection and forensic child psychology: he is co-author of *Assessing Children at Risk*.

**Shirley Moyse** is an educational psychologist. Currently, she works in the Kent County Council Educational Psychology Service.

**Anna Nolan** works as an educational psychologist in the Educational Psychology Service of the London Borough of Waltham Forest.

**Graham Pratt** is a senior educational psychologist in the Educational Psychology Service of the London Borough of Waltham Forest.

**Gillian Pugh** is Director of the Early Childhood Unit at the National Children's Bureau. She has worked extensively with central and local government on the development of policy for young children, and has published widely on policy development, on the co-ordination of services, support for parents and parental involvement in early childhood services. She is Chair of the Primary Education Study Group and of the Early Childhood Education Forum and a Vice-President of the National Childminding Association.

**Professor Euan Ross** is Professor of Community Paediatrics, King's College School of Medicine and Dentistry, London and Honorary Consultant Paediatrician to King's Health Care, Maudsley Hospital and West Lambeth Community Care Trust. His clinical and research interests include child development, prevention against infectious disease and epilepsy in children.

**Philippa Russell** is Director of the Council for Disabled Children at the National Children's Bureau and an Associate Director of the National Development Team for People with Learning Disabilities. She has worked on the development of guidance on children with disabilities and special educational needs relating to both the Children Act 1989 and the Code of Practice and Education Act 1993. Lastly, but by no means least, she is the parent of a young man with learning disability and is associated with a wide range of voluntary and parent organizations throughout and beyond the United Kingdom.

**Dorothy Rouse Selleck** is a Senior Development Officer in the Early Childhood Unit at the National Children's Bureau. She has worked with children in nursery and infant schools, and for children as a consultant and as a tutor in early voluntary education. She works with educators from the education, social services and private sectors and has a special interest in how children learn, and in the curriculum for children from birth to eight years old.

**Michael Sherwin** qualified as a Solicitor in 1970. After seven years with the London Borough of Lewisham as the solicitor advising the Social Services Department, he set up in partnership with Richard White (Editor of *Clarke Hall* *and Morrison on Children*) and his firm in Croydon practises exclusively in the area of law concerning children.

**Peter M. Smith** works at the Department of Health as a Social Services Inspector and also as a guardian ad litem and child care trainer. Previously he worked at the National Children's Bureau as Principal Policy Officer where he was closely involved in amendments to the Children Bill. He has published a number of articles about the Children Act, child witnesses and child protection.

**Professor Graham Upton** is Pro-Vice Chancellor of the University of Birmingham where he is also Professor of Special Education and Educational Psychology. He has taught in ordinary and special schools, and been involved in teacher education for over twenty years. In addition, he has conducted individual and large scale funded research and written widely on many aspects of special education.

**Dr Ved Varma** was an educational psychologist with the London Boroughs of Richmond and Brent until he retired. He is an experienced teacher and has worked at the Tavistock Clinic in London as an Educational Psychologist. He has extensive editorial experience having previously edited, or co-edited, sixteen books.

# Index